dig in

Outdoor STEM Learning with Young Children

Lea Ann Christenson, PhD, and Jenny James, MA

Gryphon House
www.gryphonhouse.com

Copyright

Library of Congress Control Number: 2022934702

Bulk Purchase

Gryphon House books are available for special premiums and sales promotions as well as for fund-raising use. Special editions or book excerpts also can be created to specifications. For details, call 800.638.0928.

Disclaimer

Gryphon House, Inc., cannot be held responsible for damage, mishap, or injury incurred during the use of or because of activities in this book. Appropriate and reasonable caution and adult supervision of children involved in activities and corresponding to the age and capability of each child involved are recommended at all times. Do not leave children unattended at any time. Observe safety and caution at all times.

Table of Contents

Introduction

Let us introduce ourselves. I'm Lea Ann Christenson. Currently, I am an Associate Professor in the Department of Early Childhood Education at Towson University in Maryland. My career in education started as a kindergarten teacher at a public school in the Santa Cruz Mountains of California. A Life Lab class garden was a regular part of the school's curriculum—we offered hands-on science, technology, engineering, and math instruction before the term *STEM* was coined. I also taught first and second grade and English as a second language and served as an assistant principal of an elementary school before moving to Maryland, where I earned my doctorate in curriculum and instruction, with an emphasis on early literacy. Over the past ten years, I have had opportunities to collaborate and conduct research and to offer professional development with educators in the United States, Denmark, El Salvador, Zimbabwe, Nepal, and China.

I'm Jenny James. I am an early childhood advocate, author, and director of a Lutheran school in Maryland, where I use STEM skills daily in the administration of the preschool. Over my forty-year career, I worked as a helper in a family child-care home, a teacher in numerous child-care centers and preschools, a family counselor and project manager for a child-care resource and referral agency, and the child-care training coordinator for the state of Maryland. I strive to inspire teachers to find their inner creative, spontaneous selves so that they can deliver exciting learning experiences that they and their students will remember. My interest in outdoor learning was influenced by my own childhood experiences mixing pretend potions with water, leaves, and dirt. I remember the pride in creating something new, working with tools that grown-ups use, and the feeling that I was doing something that mattered. In my career, I have observed the transformative qualities that being outdoors brings to children and adults alike. I believe that child-led play under the guidance of a supportive teacher leads to deep, joyful learning, and I want to share that joy with the readers of this book. Like many of our readers, we share a love of teaching, teachers, children, and their families. Many teachers agree that their love of children, their own creative energy, or their desire to make a difference inspired them to choose the profession (Karakiş, 2021). However, when it comes to teaching STEM subjects, research shows that many teachers lack confidence and interest in adding STEM to their lessons (Adams et al., 2014). These feelings of uncertainty about teaching science, technology, engineering, and math, along with the unpredictable nature of outdoor learning, may keep some teachers indoors. We want to break down the barriers that deter teachers from digging into STEM, so that they can confidently embrace outdoor STEM learning. Teachers will discover the spark of STEM learning as we share how outdoor STEM education is supported by philosophers and theorists, past and present, of early childhood development. We hope this understanding will motivate teachers to see outdoor STEM learning experiences as equal partners to the typical block, art, and dramatic play experiences included in most early learning classrooms.

We contend that STEM lessons for young children are more interesting for teachers and students when those lessons are tweaked and redefined to take place outside. Consider the number of times a teacher creates a lesson plan that will take place outdoors. For most teachers, there would be very few. Why is that? Control. Indoors, teachers are trained to control the materials, room arrangement, scheduling, and messiness. This is often called "good classroom management." Administrators praise these organized environments, but some do not understand that this is not necessarily the best way for young children to learn. A wise teacher knows how to manage her class while offering opportunities for true exploration. Too often, teachers will find comfort in the control and will miss opportunities for learners to take the lead.

Are you one of those teachers? You're in good company! All teachers experience tension between exploration and the pressure to meet standards, have children pass "readiness" assessments, and maintain discipline. Think about the times that your lesson plans have gone awry. Perhaps it started to snow, and you lost your audience to the pretty flakes falling on the playground. Or maybe someone discovered a spider in the classroom while you were teaching a math lesson. In those moments, it takes flexibility for a teacher to adapt lessons to meet students where they are. Instead of going on with the planned lesson, what would happen if you taught the skills you wanted to teach through the lens of serendipitous events? These kinds of experiences are even more likely to occur outdoors, where the learning can be more meaningful and authentic and can connect to children's wonder. What do you wonder about snow? How can we find out? How many legs does the spider have? Let's count them!

It is this type of flexibility, love of wonder, and ability to adapt that is necessary to teach STEM to young children. So, if you chose the teaching profession because of your love of children, and you can embrace your own sense of wonder, then you are on your way to becoming an effective outdoor STEM teacher!

How This Book Is Organized

Can you meet standards and still nurture learners who can think critically, collaborate, communicate, and create? Yes! Using our combined experiences with children, teachers, community stakeholders, families, and student teachers, we offer teachers and administrators the tools to organize outdoor STEM lessons that promote twenty-first-century skills.

In chapter 1, we describe the richness of learning outdoors and the opportunities nature affords for STEM-based explorations. In chapter 2, we share what we call the Learning Life Cycle to use as a frame for outdoor learning. Next, in chapter 3, we explore how deep thinkers in early childhood landscapes support outdoor learning, and we show connections between indigenous ways of knowing and the prevalent theories of early childhood.

In chapter 4, you will learn how to plant the seed of experiential learning through outdoor education. Focusing on typical preschool themes, we show how to transform your lessons for the outdoors or bring nature indoors for more authentic STEM learning experiences. Chapter 5, Growing the Roots of Wonder, connects how activities such as simple observation can lead to many weeks of investigating an environmental topic chosen by your students. We walk you through the twenty-first-century skills of critical thinking, collaboration, communication, and creativity so that you can confidently add a sense of wonder to your lessons. Chapter 6, Unearthing STEM in the Learning Life Cycle, will inspire you to take STEM learning outdoors in your own unique setting or to move the outdoors in, with easily accessible materials. Journaling, charting, classifying, matching, and many other activities illustrate how teachers can support authentic learning inside and outside the classroom.

Outdoor learning is not about a state-of-the-art outdoor space. It is about putting into action instruction that embraces the natural environment. Teachers can move to more appropriate teaching of literacy and critical-thinking skills using STEM and the environment. In addition, outdoor STEM instruction can open the doors for students who are underrepresented in the STEM workforce by illuminating these disciplines at an early age and allowing them to see themselves in these fields. Chapter 7 discusses the importance of communication and stakeholder buy-in in starting an outdoor classroom. Chapter 8 provides practical ideas and tips for leveraging outdoor environments for maximum STEM learning.

In the appendices, we offer tools to help you adapt your curriculum or themes for outdoor learning and resources where you can find more ideas for rich outdoor learning. **Ready? Let's dig in!**

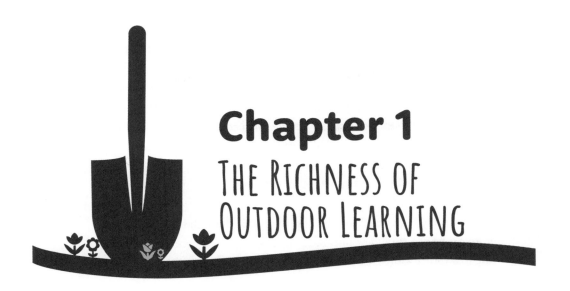

Chapter 1
THE RICHNESS OF OUTDOOR LEARNING

Outdoor Learning Honors the Whole Child

Outdoor environments are a perfect match for the unpredictable nature of STEM learning. Full-body, physical experiences happen outdoors. All the senses are stimulated: proprioception (the sense of one's body in space), vestibular (balance), hearing, sight, smell, taste, and touch. (By the way, the development of these are precursors to emergent literacy skills. We'll get to that in a moment.) Outdoor experiences naturally lead to collaboration because they inspire movement and the sharing of ideas. Where some children are comfortable verbally sharing ideas, others may be more comfortable participating through movement, which is much more acceptable and authentic outdoors—think of the times when you struggle with discipline in your classroom. You may be hesitant to move outdoors because you think you might lose control of the children. The opposite is likely to happen when children are engaged in movement and child-driven lessons. In his feature article "Outdoors for All: Access to Nature Is a Human Right," Richard Louv (2021) presents the following:

> Expanding research has also shown that exposure to nature can reduce children's symptoms of attention deficit hyperactivity disorder and help prevent or reduce obesity, myopia, and vitamin D deficiency. And the research suggests that time spent in nature may improve social bonding and reduce violence, stimulate learning and creativity, help raise standardized test scores, and serve as a buffer to toxic stress, depression, and anxiety.

Moving outdoors also removes the problem of deafening acoustics—an indoor classroom can get noisy when young children are busy learning. The noise can be a barrier to some learners (and teachers). Having class outdoors allows for children to raise their voices and move, reaching more children with a wide variety of strengths: kinesthetic, verbal, artistic, and scientific. The outdoor environment will challenge the physicality of the sedentary learner and pique the interest of the active child.

Outdoor experiences give more freedom for children of different abilities to show what they know and enthusiastically add to their knowledge base. These experiences naturally lead to differentiated instruction for children who are differently abled or are dual language learners, so that they too can show their many strengths. Outdoor lessons are hands-on, authentic experiences; a knowledge of English is not necessary to meet with success.

Outdoor Explorations and Language Learning

Through doing and not just listening, children build conceptual knowledge and academic vocabulary that are the foundation of critical thinking and literacy

acquisition (Shechter, Eden, and Spektor-Levy, 2021). For example, if children are engaged in outdoor water play, building bridges and moats and dams in the mud, they might not have the vocabulary yet for the things they are building. However, they have the conceptual knowledge of what each construction does to the flow of water. Under the guidance of a skillful teacher who narrates what the children are doing and provides the academic vocabulary to describe the events, all children can understand the underlying principles.

Through these types of activities, dual language learners will retain the conceptual knowledge and add English vocabulary as they become more fluent. Hands-on experiences provide conceptual knowledge to build language. A child who has a rich academic vocabulary and understanding of the world is more likely to meet with academic success in the future (Ramsook, Welch, and Bierman, 2020). Outdoor lessons are a path to this success.

Outdoor Explorations and Social-Emotional Learning

Outdoor opportunities support social-emotional learning (SEL) as well. Despite recent pushes in early education to teach more academics using worksheets and drills, a large body of research supports including SEL in educational programs (Mahoney, Durlak, and Weissberg, 2018). With an increased awareness of the importance of a child's emotional health, many child-care settings and schools have adopted programs to foster SEL. These programs cannot be effective, however, if SEL is limited just to a unit of study; SEL should be incorporated into every aspect of a young child's day. The major aspects of SEL—self-awareness, self-management, social awareness, relationship skills, and responsible decision making (Durlak et al., 2011)—can be authentically achieved in an outdoor-education setting infused with STEM.

SEL is about being confident, solving problems, learning from mistakes, and working with others. As you read this book, keep the principles of SEL in mind and think about how the activities foster SEL while building critical-thinking skills and meeting the required curriculum standards.

Outdoor Learning Supports Pre-K Standards

Over the past twenty years, there has been a movement toward accountability-based teaching to make sure no learners are "left behind." The result has been an assessment-driven curriculum and methods that are not appropriate for young children. What was once expected of first- or second-graders is now, in many cases, expected of four-year-olds. The good news is that taking learning outdoors is a way to meet these standards in a developmentally appropriate manner.

Like their indoor counterparts, teachers who teach outside need a conceptual understanding of the curriculum standards and objectives so that they can adapt their lessons to meet the interests of their students. For those of you who are new to outdoor learning, understand that you will have a plan, but you will also be looking for ways to teach children how to explore their interests and address their wonders through the STEM subjects. You will, in effect, be showing students the importance of STEM in the way that you guide their learning about the outdoor environment. In addition, outdoor education can cover the required acquisition of benchmark skills in content areas such as social studies, music, and art, all while engaging students in environmental study.

LITERACY ACQUISITION

One of the most important areas of instruction in the early childhood classroom is literacy. The method for literacy instruction in the early grades is also possibly the most misunderstood. Over the past twenty years, literacy instruction in early childhood has focused more on rote skills, such as learning sight words, which

have little support in the research. So, what are some of the best practices around literacy instruction? Would you guess gross-motor activities?

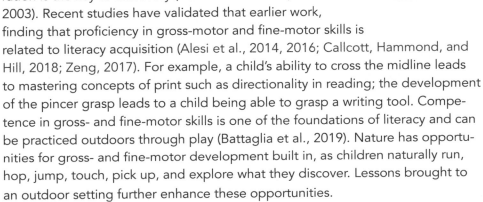

Psychologist Jean Piaget developed a theory of how children develop intellectually. His cognitive development theory, in part, posited that a child's motor development allows the child to explore the world, and consequently, that exploration is the key to discovery (Huitt and Hummel, 2003). Recent studies have validated that earlier work, finding that proficiency in gross-motor and fine-motor skills is related to literacy acquisition (Alesi et al., 2014, 2016; Callcott, Hammond, and Hill, 2018; Zeng, 2017). For example, a child's ability to cross the midline leads to mastering concepts of print such as directionality in reading; the development of the pincer grasp leads to a child being able to grasp a writing tool. Competence in gross- and fine-motor skills is one of the foundations of literacy and can be practiced outdoors through play (Battaglia et al., 2019). Nature has opportunities for gross- and fine-motor development built in, as children naturally run, hop, jump, touch, pick up, and explore what they discover. Lessons brought to an outdoor setting further enhance these opportunities.

Oral-Language Development

Oral language is the foundation of reading and writing. Children who have rich vocabularies are better readers and writers when they are older (Chang et al., 2020; Reed and Lee, 2020). Teachers need to provide ample time during the day for children to have deep conversations, not lectures, on topics that are of interest to them. Teachers also need to scaffold children to greater levels of understanding. Embedded in oral-language instruction are learning to be good listeners and the ability to express oneself. Hands-on experiences based on children's interests give children interesting topics and conceptual knowledge to discuss with each other and with their teachers. STEM-focused lessons give children plenty of opportunities to record their data and report their findings through shared oral presentations.

A consistent body of research over time shows that a rich and deep understanding of the world around us helps children become better readers both in the higher grades and as adults. With that understanding, individuals are able to develop a large academic vocabulary (Duff, Tomblin, and Catts, 2015). Reading is not just about the ability to decode words. It is about the ability to comprehend and think critically about what is read and then to apply it to life. Children who have many hands-on experiences in real-life situations walk away with an understanding of the world and the words to describe it.

Mirrors and Windows

Rudine Sims Bishop introduced the concept of mirrors and windows in reference to selecting multicultural books (Moir, 1990). In her essay, she suggests that books should be mirrors that reflect the culture of children and should be windows to show children other cultures (Moller, 2016). She also suggests that books could be sliding doors that allow children to walk into a story and become a part of the world the author has created (Moller, 2016).

Like books, outdoor activities can provide mirrors and windows for young scientists. When teachers prepare lessons in outdoor environments, along with materials that reflect each child, they show them a window to the wider world. With hands-on activities children can literally step into that world. In this way, all children can develop self-efficacy and can see themselves as innovators and problem solvers who use language to describe and share their ideas.

Schemas

Piaget and others theorized that children create schemas to understand how the world works. A *schema* is a structure used to explain what we observe. Learners develop academic vocabularies around schemas. For example, after a hands-on unit about firefighters (see chapter 3), the children will develop a schema around what firefighters do and will build vocabulary to describe what they do. Later, when a child is reading a book and encounters the word *fire* or *fighter,* she will connect to the schema of firefighters and have access to all she has learned through hands-on experiences.

Whether learning about firefighters, the weather, fairy tales, or the life cycle of a butterfly, the learning is all about building schemas and the academic vocabulary to describe them. Vocabulary memorized and taught out of context tends to be forgotten pretty quickly and has little use. Children who have opportunities to learn outdoors around themes suggested by the teacher will learn new vocabulary in context, a process that will yield better readers later in life.

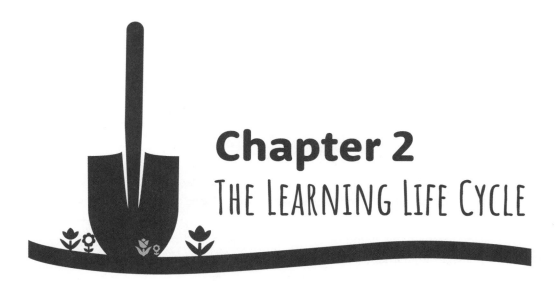

Chapter 2
The Learning Life Cycle

Outdoor STEM learning is an integral part of what we call the Learning Life Cycle. This life cycle includes four phases:

→ **Outdoor Experiences:** Seeds
→ **Wonder:** Roots
→ **STEM:** The Stem That Supports the Growth of the Plant
→ **Creative Expression:** Flowers, Leaves, Fruit

The Learning Life Cycle is a guide for teachers to use as they develop outdoor lessons that support children's learning through play and exploration. We have seen how childlike wonder can inspire deep learning, and we hope to inspire you to identify it in your own programs. The STEM subjects are best taught in context with meaning, and we will show you how nature and outdoor play can bring that context to STEM learning. Discover how your students can share and celebrate newfound knowledge using language arts, social studies, and creative arts. Using the Learning Life Cycle as a reference point, you can gain a better understanding of where your students are in their own individual learning. You will learn how

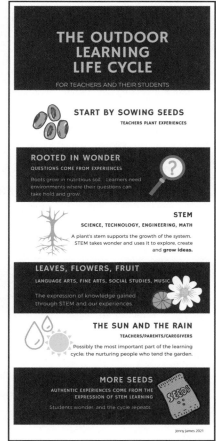

THE OUTDOOR LEARNING LIFE CYCLE

FOR TEACHERS AND THEIR STUDENTS

START BY SOWING SEEDS

TEACHERS PLANT EXPERIENCES

ROOTED IN WONDER

QUESTIONS COME FROM EXPERIENCES

Roots grow in nutritious soil.   Learners need environments where their questions can take hold and grow.

STEM

SCIENCE, TECHNOLOGY, ENGINEERING, MATH

A plant's stem supports the growth of the system. STEM takes wonder and uses it to explore, create and **grow ideas.**

LEAVES, FLOWERS, FRUIT

LANGUAGE ARTS, FINE ARTS, SOCIAL STUDIES, MUSIC

The expression of knowledge gained through STEM and our experiences.

THE SUN AND THE RAIN

TEACHERS/PARENTS/CAREGIVERS

Possibly the most important part of the learning cycle: the nurturing people who tend the garden.

MORE SEEDS

AUTHENTIC EXPERIENCES COME FROM THE EXPRESSION OF STEM LEARNING

Students wonder, and the cycle repeats.

Jenny James 2021

to dive deeper into outdoor learning by allowing your students to go through each of the four phases. Each child will enter the phases at different times, depending on how he experiences nature. The teacher's role is that of guide and mentor. Consider, "What experiences am I giving my students today?" or "Am I allowing time for wondering?" When children have access to the outdoors and nature, together with a supportive teacher, they will become active participants in the Learning Life Cycle.

Outdoor learning has a unique rhythm. Unlike the indoor classroom environment that is basically the same day after day, season after season, the outdoors is ever changing, creating new challenges and opportunities. It is up to the teacher to help young learners follow the beat and the rhythm that outdoor learning provides. Armed with a lesson plan built on STEM standards, teachers can bring attention to experiences in the natural environment. Experiences, whether teacher-led or child-driven, are the first phase in the Learning Life Cycle.

Experiences: Seeds Planted in Rich Soil

The first phase in the Learning Life Cycle is planting the seeds in soil to lead to the development of strong roots. These seeds—outdoor learning experiences—foster child-driven activities, honor the whole child, and encourage risk-taking with limit setting and structure. In the article "Nature in Education," originally published in her book *The Discovery of the Child*, Maria Montessori uses the example of harvesting grain or grapes with children as a way for them to experience "the secret fascination of sowing" (Montessori, 1950; 2013). Indeed, once you start harvesting the fruits of your labor—the incredible "Aha!" learning moments of your students—you will understand what motivates teachers who sow the seeds of outdoor experiences. Lessons created with the Learning Life Cycle in mind can take place indoors; however, when moved outdoors, lessons are a much more natural and logical manifestation of this model.

From Teacher-Led to Child-Driven Experiences

In a traditional early childhood classroom, you might walk in and be greeted by a bulletin board of uniform penguins with googly eyes created by children to culminate a unit about winter. What if, instead, the teachers offered a provocation of various art materials with different textures after a discussion about coats of winter animals, so that each child could create something of his own? In this way, teachers resist the temptation to have a prototype that often represents stereotypical icons. As hard as it may be to skip the revered projects that have become institutionalized in your repertoire, we give you permission to ditch the googly-eyed penguins or craft bunnies made with cotton balls. While these projects may be cute, they leave little to the imagination or ingenuity of the children producing them. Ask yourself, "Who owns the cleverness of this activity?" If the answer is you, the activity may be too teacher focused.

Teacher-focused activities can sometimes get in the way of critical thinking. For instance, if you give your students only blue paper to create a sky, you are reinforcing the idea that the sky is blue. But is the sky *only* blue? By providing additional colors of paper, you provide an opportunity for your students to think critically about the various colors the sky can be. There is no rule, for example, that you must represent the sky with blue paper or a smiling yellow sun. When a child is given the choice of colors for a sky, and he chooses pink, orange, and yellow because he wants to portray a sunset, isn't that cleverer than everyone having a finished project with a blue sky? That simple choice has opened up a learning opportunity about the changing colors of the sky that you may not have considered—*why* does the sky change color? We contend that the experiences you offer children are like planting seeds in rich soil. So much more can be learned from a changing sky.

The previous craft activities are typical of controlled indoor settings. In contrast, experiences outdoors are more spontaneous. Children react and adjust to an environment that is constantly changing. Critical thinking is supported by the very nature of being outdoors; however, teachers still have objectives and plan experiences to meet the needs of their students. You may be wondering how teachers plan spontaneous

experiences. (Is it still spontaneous if it is planned? This is a contradiction in terms!) A child-led experience does not mean that the teacher isn't present. In fact, the teacher is more present than in some teacher-led activities. The teacher watches closely as children pay attention to different aspects of the outdoor environment and seizes the opportunities to explore the topics further. The overall experience is intentionally planned, but the *way* in which the students interact with the materials and ideas is spontaneous. This is where you will see children collaborating over a game they are inventing or choosing to collect acorns to make acorn stew. Have you ever been surprised at something a child created? Outdoor experiences lead to the best kind of surprises—the kind of surprises that make teachers and children proud of their work. These experiences are necessary for authentic "Aha!" moments.

Here is an example of how learning happens naturally outdoors, by simply providing time to play outside.

> Ms. Rose sets up the learning experience (plants the learning "seed") by allowing children to discover and play outside. As she looks across the playground, she notices four-year-old Alexa playing with mulch and sticks. Walking over, she observes that the play is intentional. Alexa wonders about how to help ants get over a puddle (her experience is taking root with wonder). She explains to Ms. Rose that she is making a bridge for ants. The question prompts her to use problem-solving skills of engineers to balance the mulch (STEM helps support the idea). Ms. Rose identifies her use of STEM by saying, "It looks like you are engineering the bridge so that the ants don't have to go around the puddle!" Alexa tells an elaborate story about the ants on the playground and their adventures in crossing the bridge. Ms. Rose takes a photograph of the ant bridge and asks Alexa to dictate a story, which Ms. Rose records. She shares the recording with Alexa's family at the next conference to show how imaginative she is and how, through her play, Alexa is meeting STEM standards.

The use of STEM in her activity prompted the interesting story about ants and their adventures on the playground (representing the flowers and leaves of the "plant," or creative expression, in the Learning Life Cycle). In this casual yet effective way, Ms. Rose was able to observe Alexa achieving the skills and processes in the Maryland State Standards' prekindergarten learning domain of science, which says that students will demonstrate the thinking and acting inherent in the practice of science (Maryland State Department of Education, 2003). She also observed the student making things with simple tools and a variety of materials. Early childhood teachers who catch moments like bridge building for ants start to see that their students are meeting state standards in meaningful ways beyond what they might have planned. And it all starts with experiences that lead to wonder.

Wonder: The Root of Discovery

What are your students experiencing outdoors today? I wonder what happened to the mud that we played with yesterday. I wonder how we could get more mud. How can we carry our leaf collection from the ground to the big rock? How do you think the cicada can hang upside down? Who or what moved the apple that had been left in the woods? All of these questions show a sense of wonder, which is at the root of all discoveries and the second phase in the Learning Life Cycle.

Communication is a key skill used in this phase of learning and is also at the heart of English language arts. Proficient readers in higher grades are children who have rich experiences and abundant academic vocabularies (words to describe topics and themes). Outdoor education is a natural conduit for communication and the development of essential literacy skills via questioning.

Teachers may take time to observe their students in the outdoor environment to see what kinds of questions come up. Any of these questions can be a jumping-off point to meeting a STEM or other standard in the curriculum. Heather B. Taylor (2019) explains in her article "From Fear to Freedom: Risk and Learning in a Forest School" what a child-led, inquiry-based curriculum looks like: "Following the children's lead helped me develop the ways of teaching I was coming to discover on my own: the environment and the children themselves do the educating. A branch breaking off a tree; muddy hillsides to climb; blackberries warmed by the sun, ready to pick and eat; a favorite toy or book a child wants to share—all represent examples of the curriculum that was ever-changing, unplanned, and ultimately meaningful." The questions that come from these types of experiences naturally lead to deeper learning.

STEM: Providing Support for Deeper Learning

Using STEM to find answers or solve problems is the third phase of the Learning Life Cycle. STEM skills are put in action outdoors and are made relevant through hands-on learning. The same critical-thinking skills that we practice in the STEM subjects can be used to think about our natural environment.

If you think of experiences as seeds that grow roots (questions), the natural progression is the growth of the stem or STEM. Wondering that takes root will lead to using science, technology, engineering, and math to find answers to our questions. This approach to learning models what lifelong learning is about. Students see that teachers also use STEM to find answers. What skills will we use to solve the problem of our sandbox flooding when it rains? What skills will we use when we classify the types of leaves we find or count the different species of birds we see? What tools will we need to study worms? (In chapter 5, we will look at how simply narrating children's play and reflecting on their actions with descriptive STEM words can help students understand that they are using STEM skills in their play.)

Creative Expression: The Fruit, Flowers, and More Seeds!

Creative expression is the fourth phase in the Learning Life Cycle. Have you ever learned a new app feature on your phone, after much trial and error, and then felt compelled to share the information with a friend? Sharing a new discovery can be in the form of a simple text, but often the big discoveries inspire people to create new ways of sharing their ideas or inventions. Poetry, writing, fine arts, video, photography, dance, and music are all ways in which people share their discoveries with the world. Technology, too, can play an important part in sharing the discovery. For example, teachers may take photos and guide children to present their findings in classroom displays or posting pictures on the school's website.

Outdoor classrooms often make space for art because the outdoors is the perfect place to allow for messes. A table set with watercolors or even mud to paint with is an open opportunity for creative expression. Clay can be used to create sculptures or replicas of living things. Young learners can be invited to gather small sticks, acorns, or pine cones and make collages or build onto their clay. An easel stocked with a variety of paint colors is a nice choice for outside creations. Squirt bottles filled with water can be a welcome tool for exciting experimentation on a warm day: "I wonder what will happen to our paintings when we squirt them with water?" Paintings left out to dry on a clothesline or clipped to a chain-link fence with clothespins will be a welcome display as families arrive to pick up their children. Sharing paintings and stories that reflect children's experiences can be the impetus to more critical thinking about social constructs and more. For example, while playing in the outdoor kitchen, one child said she was making masala. Masala is an Indian tea that, when in its dry state, looks very much like the dirt and leaves that she was stirring in a bowl. The teacher looked up the word *masala* and learned more about the tea, which then extended to a conversation with the child's mother and learning about the role that tea plays in their culture. Another example of creative expression: A teacher encouraged her preschoolers to draw maps of their outdoor

space. One group decided to draw a map that included an X to represent a hole they had dug. This hole, they had decided, was off limits. They covered the actual hole with two large sticks, saying, "X marks the spot." Their collaborative play created excitement as other children questioned why the hole was off limits and tested the boundaries of the two large sticks. These experiences, of course, led to debate about whether "X marks the spot" was truly a dangerous place or one that could be seen as a good place where treasures are found. The original map they had created could be changed to be a treasure map. Through imaginary play, the preschoolers shared their ideas about symbols and developed social constructs, represented by the maps that each child drew, about danger and treasure.

The wonder and critical thinking that happened organically in this exploration shows how the learning cycle repeats. This type of learning is asset based and meets the needs of all children of all abilities—including those who are learning English as a second language. Several of the children in the map-making class were dual language learners. They learned through the excitement of their peers, through drawing the maps, through the visual of forming an X out of two

sticks, and through listening to the discussion and loud debates. Children who were too timid to chime in during formal learning indoors took chances and participated in the debate by shouting, "Don't go there! Danger!" There was enough repetition in the play that the dual language learners could grasp concepts with little perceived effort. Children who usually were not interested in drawing were motivated to draw new maps and proudly carried them around the outdoor space. Children gifted in large-motor dexterity could shine in the environment, running back and forth with their maps to show others where to go.

The following examples show how the Learning Life Cycle can help you break down your lessons into manageable sections. If you remember to include the four phases of the Learning Life Cycle, you will have a well-rounded lesson that can be used both indoors and out. Take a look at the following examples of outdoor activities using loose parts, and consider how creating a child-driven lesson could follow the Learning Life Cycle.

Obstacle Course

Guide young learners in the design and execution of an obstacle course.

Phase One: Experiences

Use the story *We're Going on a Bear Hunt* by Rosen and Oxenbury (2003) to familiarize the students with the concept of an obstacle course. Have them act out the different parts of the story so that they experience the story kinetically and start to understand how an obstacle course can represent a bear hunt.

Phase Two: Wonder

The experience in setting up the activity is guided by the teacher, but the end result should reflect the work of the participants. Children will come up with a variety of ideas. The teacher's role here is as a guide. Are the ideas safe? Help your students build on their ideas to achieve something they can manage themselves. By asking questions, you lead the discussion and model what it's like to brainstorm an idea. Write down their answers and refer to them as they build the obstacle course. Ask questions such as the following:

→ How could we make an obstacle course and go on a bear hunt with what we find outside?

→ What tools, technology, and loose parts should we use to create the obstacles?

→ Is there something that we could walk or jump over safely?

→ How will we keep time?

→ How will people know where to start and end?

→ How do we want people to move through our obstacle course? run? walk? hop?

→ Where should the stations be placed?

→ How many directional signs will be needed, and how will we decide who will make them?

→ How many turns will everyone get?

→ Will there be a bear at the end of the obstacle course—or something else?

Phase Three: STEM

Assembling the obstacle course requires organization, collaboration, creativity, communication, as well as body strength, balance, and movement. Learners think critically about the best place to build their obstacle course. They count the number of stations and decide the order they should be in. They build structures for balancing and make signs to show direction. They discuss why and how to rearrange the stations and experiment with the height and weight of stepping stones. They use a stopwatch to time each other and talk about how seconds make up minutes. They are learning STEM concepts and meeting the following pre-k standards—through their *play*.

→ **Science**

* Demonstrate the thinking and acting inherent in the practice of science.

* Explore cause and effect.

- ➜ **Technology**
  - Use tools such as a scale or stopwatch/timer.

  - Using a tablet or cell phone, record children using the obstacle course.

  - Use tools such as crayons, markers, tape, and paper to make signs.

- ➜ **Engineering**
  - Explore building balance structures that are safe.

  - Design the obstacle course using loose parts.

- ➜ **Math**
  - Count to tell the number of objects.

  - Understand addition as putting together and adding to, and understand subtraction as taking apart and taking from.

  - Recognize the concept of *just before a given number* in a counting sequence (Maryland State Department of Education, 2003).

PHASE FOUR: CREATIVE EXPRESSION

The learners are much more motivated to try an obstacle course that they create themselves. They imagine swimming from one obstacle to the next. They are using positional words and new vocabulary. With the help of their teacher, they make up their own story involving the obstacle course. They call it "Going on an Octopus Hunt," incorporating their own under-the-sea adventure. This becomes one of their favorite activities, and they invent new stories throughout the school year.

This obstacle-course learning experience covers many early learning standards in addition to STEM. For example, it provides opportunities to build listening and speaking skills that are foundational to oral-language development, comprehension and application of literary text, and academic vocabulary. In addition, it offers opportunities to develop number recognition, one-to-one correspondence, and computational skills. The opportunities to practice cooperation and community-building are integral to social-emotional learning.

A Butterfly Release

At a butterfly-release ceremony outdoors, the preschoolers are excited to see that the butterflies do not automatically fly out of the net as soon as the teacher opens it. The teacher asks, "What do you think we could do to get them to come out?" One child suggests that she tip the net on its side to make it easier for the butterflies to find their way. After trying that suggestion without any results, another child shouts with authority, "No! They only fly up!" The teacher settles the net upright and tests that suggestion as well, without any luck. After a few minutes, the teacher wonders aloud if the butterflies are slow to move because they are getting used to the new colder temperature (it is much warmer in the classroom). From the teacher wondering aloud, the children are given another element to think about, which expands their understanding of the world.

The vignette gives a snapshot of the learning happening during a butterfly release. Here is a breakdown of how the Learning Life Cycle was present in the lesson.

Phase One: Experience

The young children in this example were introduced to learning about butterflies through the hands-on experience of observing real caterpillars. They had watched as the caterpillars ate and grew and then made their chrysalises.

Phase Two: Wonder

On release day, the teacher modeled the second phase of the Learning Life Cycle by asking questions such as, "What could we do to get them to come out?" "Why are the butterflies moving so slowly?" and "What is different about the temperature inside our school compared to outside?"

Phase Three: STEM

Young children practiced scientific thinking in the observation of the butterflies' development by using the technology of magnifying glasses and sketching pictures of the caterpillars. They also measured the caterpillars to see if they were growing. They used math to count the number of chrysalises that formed at the top of the caterpillar container and to compare that number to the original number of caterpillars. They discussed why the caterpillars and chrysalises are in a container with holes for air to get through. On release day, the teacher referred to the temperature and weather, both related to science and math. Engineering and problem solving are evident in the suggestion to change the position of the netting.

Phase Four: Creative Expression

After the butterfly release, the children used creative expression to share the experience through stories and art. They wondered how their butterflies would survive in the wild. This led to a new study about plants and predators, and the Learning Life Cycle starts again.

The butterfly release learning experience covers many early learning standards in addition to STEM:

- → **Literacy:** builds listening and speaking skills foundational to oral-language development, academic vocabulary
- → **Social Studies:** cooperation and community-building as part of social-emotional learning

Loose Parts

Adding loose parts is a good way to start offering provocations, which help inspire students to construct knowledge. If you have an outdoor classroom, you may set it up with an art area, reading area, climbing area, and outdoor kitchen or science lab. With your help, your students will have opportunities to use the loose parts to creatively problem solve and think critically about their environment. For instance, by adding plastic lids to the outdoor science table, children might choose to use them as small trays to store small stones that they collect. The art area can have an assortment of leaves or acorns that children can arrange and glue on a piece of wood or paper plate. Plastic bottles can be used to fill with dirt, sand, or other small objects. Recycled paper-towel rolls can be used as viewfinders to inspect small areas. If you can't think of what to do with a recycled item, don't worry! Children will often find a creative use for any object, especially when outside. To celebrate the ingenuity that comes from child-led experiences, consider adding any of these loose parts to your outdoor centers:

- → recycled caps or lids from bottles or jars
- → recycled plastic bottles
- → acorns
- → old tires
- → small rocks
- → ice-pop sticks

- pine cones
- shells
- mulch
- variety of flowers, both potted and dried
- marbles
- keys
- nuts and bolts
- paints and water for mixing
- different types of paintbrushes
- crates
- netting, scarves, or fabrics
- balls of different sizes
- PVC pipes

In chapter 2, we review philosophies from deep thinkers on developmentally appropriate practice for young children and consider how their theories relate to the Learning Life Cycle. With an emphasis on indigenous populations, we show how nature has played a starring role in the education of young children. Simply changing your mindset to encourage critical thinking can be seen as provocative; however, critical thinking and wonder are important to motivate students to learn using STEM. A teacher who delights in wonder with his students will create an environment with plenty of opportunities to practice STEM.

Questions for Reflection and Action

- How do your own childhood memories of learning outside influence your current attitudes toward teaching outdoors?
- Do you remember as a child when a teacher brought nature inside the classroom? What was the lesson about? What did you learn? How were science, technology, engineering, and math used in your discovery?
- How do you use STEM in your daily life?
- What elements of the Learning Life Cycle are you familiar with? How have you implemented them with your young learners?
- What elements of the Learning Life Cycle were new to you? How might you make them a part of your lessons moving forward?

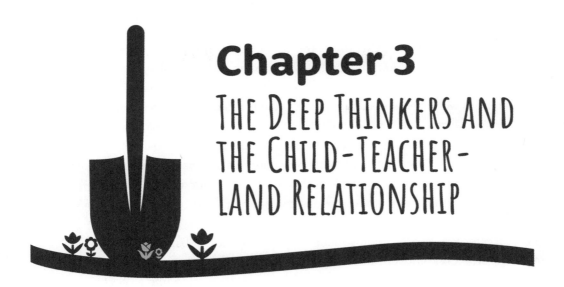

Chapter 3
The Deep Thinkers and the Child-Teacher-Land Relationship

In the New Zealand bush, an explorer program of the indigenous Maori people welcomes children ages three and four years old to explore the land through play. One participant, a four-year-old girl named Emily, enjoys climbing trees. Her teacher describes Emily's experiences in looking for spiders or cobwebs in the tree: "Later she realized there were ladybugs, bugs, and ants underneath the bark" (Okur-Berberoglu, 2021). While observing the insects, Emily peeled the bark off and tried to understand where they were traveling. Later, her mother credited her ability to make keen observations to her time spent in unstructured outdoor play.

In Ophiri Bay, New Zealand, a researcher wrote this beautiful observation of a two-year-old girl from an aboriginal community playing with stones (Malone and Moore, 2019):

> She rubbed them, piled them, and buried them in sand. She smoothed them with her thumbs. She placed them in water. She washed them. She held them close to her heart and sat on them. She sat with stones, and the more stones she encountered, the more relaxed her body and stance became. She tuned in to thinking through stones.

These examples of outdoor play and exploration meet STEM objectives and generate excitement about the environment and learning. They are also examples of the first phase of the Learning Life Cycle: child-driven experiences. The experiences described took place over several days, for at least an hour each day.

Unfortunately, when young children enter formal schooling, we may not see lessons that harness children's natural curiosity in the same interesting fashion. And when a child's natural curiosity isn't tapped, the intellectual spark that children are born with can be extinguished. It's as if the classroom itself, with its four walls, desks, posters, and school bells, dampens the deep, exciting, prideful moments of learning (Mika and Stewart, 2018). Strict school schedules don't make allowances for the time it takes to experiment and reach those "Aha!" moments. Children are transitioning from class to class without experiencing a chance to wonder, grow, and nurture a new idea, as can happen in unstructured outdoor exploration.

Jean-Jacques Rousseau, a philosopher and writer in the 1700s, wrote, "The most important and most useful rule in education is not to save time, but to waste it" (Elkind, 2015). Rousseau's rule means that, for exploration to occur, one needs time. Exploration cannot be rushed if curiosity is to grow. Deep learning happens in the space of what some might call wasted time. This philosophy connects with indigenous peoples' philosophies on outdoor education as well as those of other deep thinkers throughout history. In this chapter, we look at how indigenous people and prominent education theorists answer three philosophical questions:

- ➡ Who is the child?
- ➡ What is the role of the teacher?
- ➡ What is the role of the land?

The insights in this chapter support the Learning Life Cycle and, we hope, will inspire educators to continue the deep thinking necessary to offer children in their schools a rich and rewarding environment in which to learn. The deep thinkers named in this book are not inclusive of all the contributors to early childhood theory; however, they are connected to outdoor learning in ways that you might not have considered. We invite you to dig in and discover the relevancy of outdoor play across time and space.

Who Is the Child?

INDIGENOUS WAYS OF KNOWING

Indigenous people view children as naturally strong, equal members of society. The *Indigenous Early Learning and Child Care Framework* (2018) states that indigenous children are sacred gifts, and they must be treated as such. "Elders tell us that children are to be seen as gifts from the Creator to love, nurture, and respect" (Robertson, 2019). Most important for indigenous peoples is the child's

identity, dependent on the inclusion of culture and tradition, as well as the inclusion of the development of their spiritual, emotional, social, and physical aspect (Robertson, 2019). According to James and colleagues (2019), the Déné indigenous people in Canada believe children are born with integrity and worth, and they should be respected for this. Indeed, student agency is a valued concept in communities that honor a child's right to act autonomously and make her own decisions.

Children in the bush of New Zealand are seen as confident and competent learners from birth throughout their whole lives (Okur-Berberoglu, 2021). Their learning process consists of meaningful interactions with people and places. Malone and Moore (2019), in their observational study of aboriginal children, see them as sensorial communicators with humans and nonhumans alike. Indigenous peoples' ways of knowing is congruent with sensorial knowing, evident in their stories of animals and spirits co-existing. For example, sensorial communication with the earth and animals occurs in the sound of wind blowing through the trees, the sound and taste of the ocean, the warmth of the sun, the power of a storm, the look in the eye of a deer startled by a human presence, or a bird that rests on a fence outside a window. What is the Earth communicating? How could you respond? There is a spiritual attribute to this philosophy, which is prominent in philosophies from many of the deep thinkers, including Friedrich Froebel.

FRIEDRICH FROEBEL AND THE WHOLE CHILD

Friedrich Froebel was an educator born in Germany in 1782. His interests moved between nature and education, and he coined the term *kindergarten* (literally "children's garden") (McNair and Powell, 2020). Froebel's philosophy about the child mirrors that of indigenous people's ways of knowing, in that he saw the purpose of life as "to attain a unity of self, society, nature, universe, and spirit" (Elkind, 2015). He thought that children should live in harmony with nature (Tovey, 2017). Froebel wanted his kindergartens to support the whole child, which meant that they would support active, curious, and creative learners. Outdoor STEM education supports Froebel's idea that a child naturally observes and analyzes the world: "Question after question comes out of his inquiring mind—How? Why? When? What for?" (Tovey, 2017). Wondering, observing, and analyzing connect to the wonder and STEM phases of the Learning Life Cycle. In Froebel's view, the child is part of humanity, humanity is part of nature, and, therefore, part of the universe (Elkind, 2015). Unfortunately, in the U.S. educational system, this holistic way of thinking did not take root in grades past kindergarten. Schools were, and some still are, entrenched in didactic teaching, including a big emphasis on memorization of facts. John Dewey, a deep thinker who honored the whole child, worked to transform the teacher-led curriculum in America into a child-driven one.

DEWEY AND THE CHILD'S INTERESTS

John Dewey was born in Vermont in 1859 and was a well-known educational reformer of his era. He wanted to change the education system from indoor didactic classroom instruction to a more social approach, in which children would wander in and out of the classroom depending on their interests. Because of his pragmatic philosophy, he is also known as one of the founders of outdoor learning. He believed that children's own instincts, activities, and interests should be the starting point of education (*Early Childhood Today*, 2000).

Dewey analyzed children's curiosity as moving through three parts:

- → Energetic physical explorations
- → Questioning and investigations of social curiosity
- → More sustained and systematic problem solving of intellectual curiosity (Luff, 2018)

You can see these three stages represented in the play of the children in the "X marks the spot" scenario described on page 17. They had dug a hole, which took physical endurance and energy. They then drew maps and questioned whether the spot was dangerous or held a secret treasure. Their play led to drawing more maps and sustained play that included marking the spot with sticks in the shape of an X. These three phases correspond to the Learning Life Cycle as well: experience, wonder, and using STEM to solve problems. The three parts also correspond with the way Maria Montessori saw children as active participants in their own learning.

MONTESSORI AND THE STRONG CHILD

Maria Montessori was an extraordinary woman with strong opinions about outdoor learning. Born in 1870, she was the first female physician in Italy (Elkind, 2015). Like Froebel, the centerpiece of her philosophy is that education should consider the whole child—her mental, spiritual, physical, emotional, and social ways of being. In "Nature in Education," she describes young children as stronger than we can imagine and says their strength is revealed through free play and being outdoors (Montessori, 2013). She gives the example of a toddler walking miles on the beach, "their tireless little legs climbing steep slopes in the sunshine" (Montessori, 2013). That physical activity is central to her ideas that children find their greatest pleasure in acting, knowing, and exploring. Echoing indigenous ways of thinking she says, "A child needs to live naturally and not simply have a knowledge of nature." Further, she equates the child's intellect and observation skills to those of poets: "Only poets and little children can feel the fascination of a tiny rivulet of water flowing over pebbles" (Montessori, 2013). This connection is reminiscent of the indigenous peoples who see children as sensorial communicators with humans and non-humans. Maria Montessori saw the intellect in a child playing in a stream. This same type of investigative play informed Piaget's early learning theory.

PIAGET AND THE PLAYFUL CHILD

In the early 1900s, some people believed that children are less skilled at thinking than adults (Redford, 2013). Psychologist Jean Piaget viewed the child as centered on herself and capable of spontaneous ideas about the world. The child is at the center of learning, and activities are play-based. His theory is like the indigenous Déné elders' philosophy that play is essential to learning (James, Dragon-Smith, and Lacey, 2019).

Piaget introduced the concept of children developing toward the stage where they can reason and use hypotheses in their thinking. He categorized children's development into four stages:

→ Sensorimotor (birth to two years old): learning through the senses and movement

→ Preoperational (two to seven years old): developing language and symbolic play

→ Concrete operational (seven to eleven years old): developing logical thought

→ Formal operational (eleven years old and up): developing abstract thought

Children in the preoperational stage might learn about science by imagining what it is like to change into a butterfly or creating a "recipe" of their own design from outdoor materials. While these lessons ring true for many educators as developmentally appropriate, not all theorists and educators believe that children should be defined by the four stages of development. Still, the concept of learning through play has remained a widely accepted philosophy among early childhood professionals and across early learning theories.

MALAGUZZI AND THE CHILD WITH A HUNDRED LANGUAGES

Loris Malaguzzi was an educator, administrator, and activist known for his leadership in starting a network of public schools for young children in Reggio Emilia, Italy (Moss, 2016). The Reggio Emilia approach is a result of his work and the community that supported it. He saw children as rich with a hundred languages, meaning that children had many ways of expressing themselves and relating to the world through art, music and dance, math, science, and technology (Moss, 2016). Malaguzzi's view of children said that "children are not only complex and holistic beings, but competent and determined from birth to make meaning of the world" (Moss, 2016). He saw children as equals with rights, values, and competencies. You can see his passion for community in his desire to bring social justice to children and families in the city of Reggio Emilia through the development of meaningful educational opportunities.

VYGOTSKY AND THE CHILD APPRENTICE

Lev Vygotsky, a psychologist born in the same year as Piaget, argued that learning happens through social interactions. People learn with the help of a "knowledgeable other" via scaffolding in their *zone of proximal development* (ZPD) (Vygotsky, 1978). The ZPD is the sweet spot where the learning is too hard to do alone, but with a framework of support, the learning is possible. Teachers (the "knowledgeable others" in early childhood settings) know each of their students' abilities well and know how to scaffold them to the next level of under-standing. This type of learning is hands-on in nature; it is not about memorizing facts but about gaining a rich understanding of concepts, so learners can use what they learn in new situations. In Vygotsky's view, the role of the child is as an apprentice and role of the teacher is as a mentor.

Next, we discuss the role of the teacher according to more of our deep thinkers. As you read, ask where you see yourself in your own role as teacher. Are you a follower of one thinker? Do you subscribe to a combination of theories? What is your role as teacher?

What Is the Role of the Teacher?

INDIGENOUS PEOPLE

For indigenous people, learning is understood to be a life-long experience. In his article "Mentoring the Natural Way: Native American Approaches to Education" (2007), McClellan Hall describes Native American teachers as facilitators and members of the community sharing the responsibility of teacher. The organized system of education holds elders in high regard, as they are the teachers of traditional knowledge and carriers of the family history. Other

members of the tribe play roles as well. Because the traditional ways are generally egalitarian, men and women, aunts and uncles, and all community members are seen as mentor teachers. Hall describes the traditional Native American approaches to education as experiential: learning by doing, watching, listening, and experimenting. Scholar Gloria Ladson-Billings (2020), in her work teaching teachers how to practice culturally relevant instruction, says that relevancy should address what children need now.

This describes how many indigenous people saw education. Their education approaches were based on context (what was happening in the environment and community) and relationships. In this view, teachers must understand that knowledge is holistic, personal, social, and dependent on ecosystems. The role of the elder is to guide in the development and transmission of knowledge (James, Dragon-Smith, and Lahey, 2019). For example, in one activity, an elder-educator led a group of Inuit children out to the land where they searched for *avaalaqiat* (willow branches) to prepare branch backpacks. The concepts of *tukisiumainq*, which means "building understanding or making meaning in life," and *silatuniq*, which means "experiencing the world," are both evident in the backpack activity (James, Dragon-Smith, and Lahey, 2019).

In the indigenous Maori people's philosophy, the responsibilities of adult leaders in the bush of New Zealand are to promote a safe environment and to follow and support the children's play (Okur-Berberoglu, 2021). The New Zealand early education curriculum is named *Te Whāriki*, which means "mat for all to stand on" (Okur-Berberoglu, 2021). The curriculum has four principles: empowerment, holistic development, family, and community relationships. The teacher as follower and observer complements the sensorial approach to learning, which requires slow, uninterrupted, body-focused encounters (Malone and Moore, 2019). Sensorial learning happens when teachers step back and allow children time in and with nature. The practice of teaching as facilitator, through instruction, leading, suggesting, and scaffolding, can get in the way of sensorial learning. While not all indigenous people address holistic development in the same way, they all value family and community relationship-building as central to the role of teacher. Indigenous people value curiosity as a necessary characteristic for individual development and exploration. Their curiosity and wonder about experiences in their world give root to critical thinking, the second phase of the Learning Life Cycle.

Unfortunately, history shows that societies have repeatedly worked against the critical thinking that coincides with curiosity. Gurholt and Sanderud (2016) write, "During the European Middle Ages, church leaders and philosophers stigmatized the idea of curiosity. They feared that people who used their own eyes, ears, and voice to ask questions and acquire knowledge would challenge traditional authorities and structures." It should be no surprise that schools for American Indians did not encourage curiosity, as the U.S. government's goal was to create a civilized society that would not challenge their authority. Webber et al. (2021) address the profound impact this had on the social and learning structures of indigenous peoples. With text-based learning at the core of Western common schools, together with the removal of American Indian children from their homes for boarding schools, the education lacked historic, local information about the land and indigenous ways of knowing about nature. The role of teacher in this sad time of history was the "all-knowing" and authoritative teacher of assimilation.

FROEBEL AND THE TEACHER AS GUIDE

While some accept play as how children learn to think about their world, others may see play as a hindrance to the knowledge a teacher can impart to her students. Froebel, himself a teacher, preferred teaching young children to teaching older children. The fact that "he enjoyed playing with children in the forest and hills more than he did teaching in the classroom" (Elkind, 2015) shows how this deep thinker concluded that teaching and learning outside is agreeable for teachers and students alike! Froebel saw the mother as the child's first teacher, and he and his wife wrote a book of nursery rhymes and songs for mothers to sing and play with their children. The teacher's role was to live *with* children, meaning participate with them in their play. In this way, the teacher's role was that of guide. This is like the facilitator role that some indigenous people favor. Froebel saw the complexity of this role and set up a training school for teachers, many of them women, which at the time was unusual. Today, there are still educators trained in his methods. Froebelian teachers sum up their role this way:

- → Observing—not ticking off stages of development or isolated achievements but taking note of what children are interested in, thinking, and feeling. Observation is much more than watching. It involves listening carefully, being open, and wanting to know more.
- → Supporting and extending children's learning by sensitive intervention through planning additional resources, new experiences, or adult support
- → Tuning in to children's own play ideas, recognizing that such play can be rambunctious and messy at times but, when supported and allowed to flourish, can be sustained, collaborative, and complex

➡ Having realistically high expectations of what children are able to do. This means knowing children well enough to decide when to be quietly watchful, when to be sensitively supportive, and when to actively intervene by joining or extending the play (Tovey, 2017)

Dewey and the Teacher as Co-Learner

Dewey favored hands-on learning; his ideas influenced the project-based model of teaching used today. For Dewey, the teacher's role was to provide worthwhile new experiences. He thought that, if teachers were open to cooperative inquiry with their students, they would learn about the natural world together. As expressed in "Pioneers in Our Field: John Dewey—Father of Pragmatism":

> When we look at early childhood classrooms today, we see children building language skills as they share snacks with classmates, learning important science concepts as they water and care for plants, and developing math skills as they cook up a special treat for lunch. All these commonplace preschool activities stem from the ideas of a forward-thinking and most uncommon man (*Early Childhood Today*, 2000).

Dewey disagreed with the idea of learning only from nature. Instead, he believed the teacher's role was to show children the consequences of nature in a meaningful way (Flores-Koulish, 2019). Many teachers still adopt this approach today. For example, bringing attention to the absence of a roof on a pretend playhouse and asking children how they will keep the rain out or offering a hands-on lesson in recycling to help the environment are pragmatic ideas that incorporate nature. In this way, the teacher is leader, using nature in context with the occupations that surround it. This is different than the traditional schools that Dewey was against, where teachers fed children "facts" about nature to be memorized without any practical application.

Montessori and the Teacher as Follower

Maria Montessori said that her childhood teachers taught in the traditional fashion, in which children learned about leaves by hearing information from a book instead of going outside to collect and examine real leaves. She describes the children in the classroom as being like "butterflies mounted on pins" (Elkind, 2015), which explains the lack of freedom she felt in the didactic classroom environment. No doubt, Montessori's unfavorable childhood memories of school motivated her to develop her own school, teaching materials, and methods.

An advocate for women and children, she opened a school for children of working-class families in 1907 (Elkind, 2015). The daily schedule she developed for her school included time for learning outdoors and caring for plants and animals. In "Nature in Education," Montessori (2013) applauds parents who allow their children to walk, following behind them instead of carrying them. In this way she places teachers in the role of followers, observing children's interests and supporting them. However, the teacher is also leader in that she is to provide her students with interesting information and motives for action. Montessori cautions teachers not to mold their students' reactions to their own, but instead to follow the children's lead to discover their real tastes and needs. This attention to freedom of thought is similar to Piaget's understanding of play being the work of the child.

Piaget and the Educative Assistant

Piaget emphasizes that the role of the adult is that of an educative assistant (Joubert and Harrison, 2021). His stages of development are fostered by hands-on, adult- and teacher-facilitated learning experiences, not didactic or rote learning. Piaget believed that teachers need to meet children where they are in their development; otherwise, the children will reject the activity because they are not developmentally ready for it (Joubert and Harrison, 2021). An example of this is teaching how to tell time. Have you ever tried to teach a preschooler about time? Time is an

abstract concept. When a child in the preoperational stage asks, "Is it time to go home?" a teacher unfamiliar with Piaget's stages of development might try to teach the young child how to tell time, pointing to the clock and talking about seconds, minutes, and hours. However, any lengthy explanation about time becomes tiresome for a child in this stage (and frustrating for the teacher), and the child is likely to reject the explanation or even walk away before the teacher has finished. An educative assistant familiar with the preoperational stage would answer the same question using the child's current knowledge and expanding on it: "Remember how yesterday we went home after we ate snack? That is when we are going home today too! First we read a story, then we have snack, then we go home." She might even point to pictures on a class schedule to give the child a visual representation of her words. In this way, she is assisting the child by helping her grasp the concept of time using symbols that she can understand. A child in the next stage, concrete operational, has already learned through play and instruction about sequencing and that symbols represent concepts. She has learned simple math skills and is developmentally ready to use logic to learn how the symbols on a clock connect to the concept of time. At this stage, it is not a waste of time teach the details of a clock. Because the child is ready, the concept can be taught quickly and will support the child's growing need to measure time. Teachers, therefore, need an understanding of the four stages of development so that they can know what concepts are appropriate for the age they are teaching. Otherwise, as Piaget points out, the lesson is rejected and the time that the teacher has put into the lesson is lost.

The educative assistant not only knows what should be taught but also how to teach it. A strong learning platform for preoperational children is dramatic play. Through dramatic play, children get to try on behaviors that they may observe in their own homes. Knowing that pretend play supports learning for young children, the teacher as educative assistant might look for ways to introduce concepts through the use of props, either indoors or outdoors. For example, if learning about measurable attributes is the goal, the teacher can add measuring tools in the kitchen area and then join in the pretend play by saying, "I need two cups of acorns for my stew." The children can learn about measuring (vocabulary, counting), but the method honors where they are developmentally, at the preoperational stage. The teacher observes her students engaged in the learning rather than dismissing it. All of these experiences build on each other and are evident in developmentally appropriate practice, which leads to spontaneous learning.

Malaguzzi and the Spontaneous Teacher

Agreeing that children are capable of spontaneous ideas, Malaguzzi wanted teachers to maintain a sense of wonder when working with young children. For teachers, his advice was to "relish uncertainty" (Moss, 2016), and he explained that uncertainty was the "motor of knowledge." Teachers who follow the Reggio Emilia–inspired philosophy use the term *provocations* to describe an open-ended activity without a prescribed outcome. A provocation is designed to stimulate ideas, initiative, and imagination among children, whether they choose to explore their ideas alone or in groups. The Reggio Emilia approach supports experiential learning, and nature abounds with opportunities for children to learn by doing. Provocations lead to child-driven lessons and experiences, which produce different outcomes from teacher-led activities. Using

provocations to set up learning experiences is a thoughtful way to begin the Learning Life Cycle. You will see examples of provocations later in this book. Provocations can help children express themselves and what they know, which leads us to Vygotsky's thoughts on language.

Vygotsky and the Supportive Teacher

For Vygotsky, language encompassed the whole body. Whole-body language incorporates hand movements and gestures, which helps us make sense of the world and form scientific concepts (Karlsson, 2017). "Children initially use concepts in a spontaneous and functional way. They talk and act upon experiences on an everyday basis, and natural phenomena are intuitively and spontaneously handled" (Karlsson, 2017). The teacher's role is to know when to help children form more abstract scientific concepts by introducing new vocabulary that supports their learning. For instance, a teacher observing a child sliding rocks down a ramp that he created out of cardboard might start up a conversation about simple machines. She could also introduce the concepts of gravity and friction. Teachers can add the educational contexts pertaining to the environment and nature, and children can discover and talk about scientific phenomena because they experience various activities linking the everyday, nature-based concepts to the scientific concepts (Karlsson, 2017). The teacher does more than provide activities; otherwise, Vygotskian theory suggests, children might not ever get to the scientific concept on their own. A slow, gradual introduction of the concept helps children connect that concept with the everyday world. Thus, a teacher must practice sensitivity in observation, knowing when to step back and when to step in to help a child see the connection between the real world and abstract thought. This is what Vygotsky calls *scaffolding*. The teacher provides supports for the learner when she is ready to move to the next level of learning. In the next section, we learn about the role of the land for the deep thinkers. What role does the land play in your learning space?

What Is the Role of the Land?

INDIGENOUS WAYS OF KNOWING

Why is nature education so important to indigenous peoples? The answer can be found in the land. Kathy Absolon, an indigenous scholar, shares her childhood experiences playing in the bush in Canada: "The absence of fences, neighbors, and physical boundaries led the way for the natural curiosities of a child to grow and be nurtured" (James, Dragon-Smith, and Lahey, 2019). Her curious nature led to exploration in the bush that resulted in growth in knowledge about the world; the lack of physical boundaries was an important aspect of her experience.

The Native American perspective is that nature is animate. "The dimensions of Earth's vitality are not to be treated as mere resources to be exploited nor harnessed to the interest of human beings at the expense of other life forms" (Robertson, 2019). Simply put, indigenous people view humans as a part of nature, rather than apart from nature (Marin and Bang, 2018). To understand indigenous peoples' relationship to land, it is helpful to know their history, which is alluded to in the description that the United Nations gives to indigenous people:

Indigenous peoples are inheritors and practitioners of unique cultures and ways of relating to people and the environment. They have retained social, cultural, economic, and political characteristics that are distinct from those of the dominant societies in which they live. Despite their cultural differences, indigenous peoples from around the world share common problems related to the protection of their rights as distinct peoples (2021).

The key in this description is the reference to a *dominant society*. The early settlers in America desired a new country on their terms. To accomplish this, they wanted to save time and speed up the assimilation process so that American Indians would be sufficiently assimilated in the span of one generation (Spring, 2016). Their method would be through education and/or extinction. Indigenous ways of knowing were not respected, and as a result, atrocities in education policy were committed quickly in the name of character-building and nationalism. Around the world, attempts have been made to deculturize Indigenous people to become like the people of the dominant culture in that area. The idea of deculturalization stems from a dominant culture believing their ways are superior to others (Spring, 2016). Additionally, the dominant culture is threatened by those who are different. Naturally, this way of thinking comes with conflict, war, and aggression. In the United States, to avoid fighting over land and experiencing more conflict, efforts were started in 1819 by Thomas L. McKenney, the U.S. Superintendent of Indian Trade, to educate indigenous people in the ways of Western culture. Education was to transform American Indians into more civilized people, and therefore, easier to control. "Conceptualizing Indians

as children, McKenney believed the key to civilizing them was schooling" (Spring, 2016). Sixty years later, in 1889, Thomas Morgan, the US Commissioner of Indian Affairs, wrote a bulletin that praised the education of American Indians, especially the efforts to control them at an early age and to seclude them from tribal influences (Spring, 2016). Perhaps most unsettling was that he advocated for early childhood education to counteract the influence of the Indian home (Spring, 2016). Since a child's first world is their home, dishonoring that influence gives the child a sense of not belonging to their homeland.

Another problem with this one-sided approach is that the dominant culture does not learn about the other culture, in this case, the culture of American Indians. Gloria Ladson-Billings (2020) notes that one way to increase cultural competency is to introduce students to more than one culture. The goal is for each student to be fluent in at least two cultures. Teachers in early childhood programs can support cultural competency by researching the indigenous culture in their location and then sharing the culture with their students. Since one way to explore indigenous people's connection to the land is to be in nature with children (Robertson, 2019), outdoor learning supports cultural competency about the indigenous people's culture in that place. Therefore, parameters that interrupt children's outdoor play have a negative impact on the indigenous worldview that children are part of the environment (James, Dragon-Smith, and Lahey, 2019). With this in mind, educators can find reason to shift from limited recess periods to more extensive time spent outdoors.

An outdoor learning framework that supports indigenous people's view of the land is called *place-based education* (PBE). PBE is a community approach to connecting young people to their natural and built environments (Webber et al., 2021). Early childhood educators will be happy to know that hands-on learning is a main component of PBE. Teachers use real-world experiences in the local community to teach language arts, math, social studies, science, and subjects across the curriculum (Webber et al., 2021). PBE has been used to teach indigenous ways of knowing pertinent to the location through indigenous education literature. Webber and colleagues (2021) write about the connection of PBE to indigenous peoples: "Outdoor education, in its literal interpretation, has existed since time immemorial as it is inherent in Indigenous communities and knowledges."

Even though outdoor education existed "since time immemorial," it has been reintroduced repeatedly. In the early twentieth century, European and Scandinavian/Norwegian reforms developed experiential learning models that encouraged discovery through self-activated play (Gurholt and Sanderud, 2016). These models took place outside in nature, and gardening was an obvious subject for teaching and learning.

Froebel and the Land as a Garden

Froebel believed that the garden offered an ideal environment for young children (Tovey, 2017). His ideas about children gardening, exploring, and playing outdoors were like those of ecologists today who propose that children's understanding of the natural world motivates them to take care of it. Tovey (2017) describes Froebel's use of land: Each child had her own small plot of land in Froebel's garden. Here she could sow seeds, tend the plants, and harvest the produce. The children could experience the rhythm of nature and see the effect of the changing seasons on the garden. Gardening helped children understand the cycles of life and death, growth and decay, in direct and meaningful ways. As you might imagine, the practical nature of tending a garden was a good match for Dewey's pragmatic philosophy.

Dewey and the Land Within

Dewey's schools allowed activities to take place outdoors in nature; as he said, "Nature is not something external to human experience, rather, humans are within and part of nature" (Luff, 2018). This philosophy connects with indigenous peoples' views of the relationship between land and people. Dewey believed that gardening "evokes wonder, freedom, patience, and action in the child and a gateway to fuller appreciation of nature" (Luff, 2018). He reported that after studying American Indians, a group of children were inspired to experiment using clay from the land (Kliebard, 2004). His ideas surrounding geography were that it was not just a subject with facts and principles but how one feels and thinks of the world (2004). Land, specifically in its natural state, was also important to Montessori's beliefs about what kinds of spaces were in the best interest of children.

Montessori and the Land as Freedom

In 1915, the government of Spain invited Maria Montessori to set up an education program in Barcelona. She was provided a building with surrounding gardens, fountains, and plenty of room for outdoor play (Elkind, 2015). This setting no doubt enhanced the learning of her students, as Montessori noted in her book *The Discovery of the Child* (1950): "A child, who more than anyone else is a spontaneous observer of nature, certainly needs to have at his disposal material upon which he can work." She spares no one in her dislike of constructed playgrounds, describing one area as a "wretched piece of property not even big enough" (Montessori, 2013). Her desire was for children to experience land space that is neither too big nor too small but is most importantly a place that offers children a sense of satisfaction interacting with nature. In her most provocative analogy, she equates urban settings to prison. "The most important thing to do is to free the child, if possible, from the ties which keep him isolated in the artificial life of a city."

Piaget and the Land as an Interactive Space

Piaget proposed that children learn through actively engaging in and with their environment (Piaget and Inhelder, 1969). Indigenous African knowledge aligns with this theory when it suggests that children learn experientially through open-ended play while being supported by their local communities. Current thinking in these communities acknowledges that children can learn through playful outdoor activities that may be a combination of performing necessary chores, such as taking care of chickens, and playing street games with their peers (Joubert and Harrison, 2021). The land provides opportunities for play and exploration that, in turn, benefits the community.

Malaguzzi and the Land as Community

According to Moss (2016), "The Reggio Emilia schools were public spaces, without boundaries, open to their neighborhoods, welcoming parents and other citizens, while reaching out into their surrounding neighborhoods." One of the important aspects of the schools is that they value all indoor and outdoor environments as spaces of learning (Moss, 2016). The land, in Malaguzzi's perspective, can be viewed as a community working together, a local cultural project of educational renewal, "a place of democracy, where multiple ideas, debate, and points of view are invited and encouraged" (Moss, 2016). Gaining freedom in the land is a concept that is woven through all the early learning theories. For Vygotsky, the land offered natural opportunities to experience the freedom of ideas through its diversity.

Vygotsky and the Land as Teacher

Vygotsky believed that children's play in nature is not only diverse, but that it provides the mechanism for many important developmental outcomes (Kahn, Weiss, and Harrington, 2018). The hands-on learning activities that happen in nature also lend themselves to children's being the knowledgeable other for their peers. Scaffolding takes place in outdoor classrooms when a child shows another child how to climb logs or where to find the rock under which the ants are living. Collaboration is evident in play when one child supports another in learning. Mastering a balance activity on a small log first before trying it on a bigger log will help children build confidence in her physical abilities, stimulate sensorial learning, and meet the needs of the whole child. In Vygotsky's world, the land can be seen as teacher, but humans are necessary as coteachers to extend the learning to reach developmental outcomes of STEM subjects.

This chapter has discussed many of the deep thinkers' ideas on outdoor learning. While these thinkers each had their own twist on early learning theory, all could be activated outdoors. In fact, most incorporated outdoor learning when it was not the norm in the dominant culture of the time. You will notice, however, that the list of experts is not an exhaustive one. A critical thinker might realize the absence of perspectives from Black, Asian, or Latinx cultures. You might also wonder, with so many female teachers in classrooms, why there are not more female deep thinkers in this chapter. We hope that by bringing these inadequacies to light, you will be inspired to dig deeper into your own culture and share what you know about the roles of the child, teacher, and land. By learning together, we will realize that we all belong and have a story to tell. The stories will add to our understanding of how children learn and ultimately will give educators confidence that outdoor learning supports children and teachers of all cultures and early learning philosophies. We will now move forward with some practical ideas for contemporary teachers to share the land with their students.

Questions for Reflection and Action

- → Which deep thinker resonates the most with you? Why?
- → Was there a deep thinker you were not familiar with before? What might you apply based on their philosophy?
- → Do you think that modern-day practices in early childhood settings threaten freedom of thought?
- → What are the indigenous cultures where your classroom is located? How can these understandings influence your work with young children?
- → How can you embrace the land as a teacher?

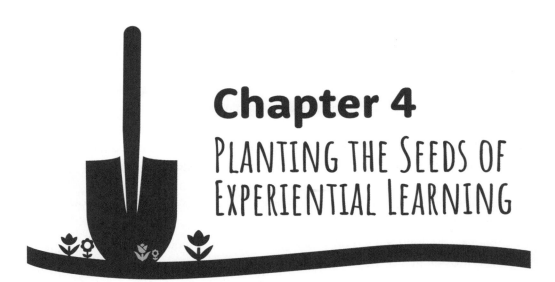

Chapter 4
PLANTING THE SEEDS OF EXPERIENTIAL LEARNING

Ms. Robyn, a seasoned teacher with years of experience in the classroom, noticed that her own strict schedule was preventing her from offering valuable learning experiences. She was planning on moving on to the next theme when she noticed that the children were more interested in playing on the playground, since the harsh winter had ended and spring days brought beautiful weather. Ms. Robyn decided to address the children's interests by extending her community-helper lessons over the course of several weeks and asking, "Does our community have any helpers who work outside?" The children began to wonder what it would be like to work outside in their community. Ms. Robyn was able to plant more experiences to help her young learners dive deeper into the subject. She placed props such as mail bags on the playground so that they could deliver mail from one climbing structure to the next. When it rained, the children decided they needed hats and umbrellas to deliver mail in the rain. The next week they pretended to be construction workers.

Changing the location of the lesson on community helpers heightened the children's outdoor exploration and ideas about their community in ways that Ms. Robyn had not planned. She found that using the outdoors to extend her unit of community helpers also dovetailed into STEM learning. Planning experiences that allow children to further explore a topic is exciting, and frankly, more authentic. Don't we see mail carriers doing their work outside? Is it not more authentic to practice delivering mail outdoors? By observing the children,

Ms. Robyn decided not to compete with the outdoors. She used the children's experiences and interest in playing outside to extend her lesson. The children's new interest in community helpers who work outside was a sign that the seeds or experiences Ms. Robyn was planting were taking root.

This chapter describes how the Learning Life Cycle helps teachers plan lessons and teach through the lens of STEM-infused, nature-based experiences. You will see examples of typical early childhood topics and how teachers transformed these topics by infusing them with STEM outdoors to teach the essential concepts of those topics in a deeper way, meet English language arts and math standards, and foster a growth mindset. Teachers find that exploring outdoor environments, whether rural, urban, or suburban, with their young learners is the easiest and most authentic way to incorporate STEM in their programs. They can do this through a structured learning unit or simply by noticing and verbally highlighting the environment while going on nature hikes, looking under rocks

for insects, observing worms in puddles, watching birds overhead, or observing leaves changing throughout the seasons. For teachers who are not comfortable teaching in an outdoor environment, start with bringing nature indoors, such as leaves that you find on a walk outside, seeds from a plant, or a branch from a tree that fell in your yard. Your students will be curious as you share something from your life outside of school with them. That curiosity can be the spark that you need to inspire your young learners. Poets, scientists, explorers, botanists, meteorologists, architects, engineers, doctors, archaeologists, athletes, and artists have all been inspired by nature. Inspiration can come from experiences outdoors or from nature coming indoors. When a teacher provides experiences for students and allows them to take the lead, exciting discoveries using STEM can take place.

Bringing the Outdoors In

It can be a luxury to have ample outdoor spaces to fully implement an outdoor, STEM-inspired classroom. Many children still do not have access to outdoor learning programs on a regular basis. The following story shows how a preschool in an urban setting still offers rich STEM experiences, even with limited access to outdoor areas.

A preschool in a large east-coast city is surrounded by streets connected by sidewalks and parking lots. It does not have an outdoor space on the campus for outside exploration. A teacher, Ms. Jasmine, and her assistant walk with the children to their local park to experience nature. While their own school's footprint is surrounded by concrete and asphalt, the children bring nature to their campus by collecting rocks, leaves, sticks, and feathers from their outdoor adventures. They place the items in a bag held by Ms. Jasmine. When they return to school, Ms. Jasmine holds up each item from the bag at the group's meeting time. She makes comments such as, "I wonder if we could see something new on this rock if we looked at it with a magnifying glass," "I wonder what kind of bird has this kind of feather," and "Why do you think the bird lost its feather?" The comments and questions give the children's outdoor excursion enhanced meaning, which then leads to STEM learning in the classroom.

The children practice science observation skills with magnifying glasses (technology). They meet math standards of sorting objects and grouping shapes by attributes as they work with a variety of different leaves and sticks. Engineering comes into play when the children figure out how they will store their new collections. They problem solve by designing boxes for each collection. Finally, with the help of Ms. Jasmine, the class writes a story together titled, "The Story of the Bird with the Missing Feather." They share the story with their families, along with a photograph of the real feather they found on their walk.

When it is not possible to be outdoors, teachers can bring the outdoors in and achieve some of the same results. These outdoor lessons brought inside will also help children meet the early learning standards in literacy and math in authentic developmentally appropriate ways. Let's take a look at how Mr. Jay brought the outdoors inside to meet early learning standards.

After a recent storm, Mr. Jay finds a small tree that has fallen near his house. He decides to bring a tree limb in so that the children in his preschool class can study it. One child says it looks like a branch that fell near his house, which leads to a discussion of the recent storm and the causes of the storm. The children then take a walk outside and to see what types of trees grow in their area and, with Mr. Jay's help, identify this specific species of tree. They use magnifying glasses to look at the insects living on the limb and record their observations in their scientific journals. As they learn more, their drawings become more detailed. The children develop rich academic vocabulary about trees, such as *bark*, *roots*, and *photosynthesis*, and develop a scientific understanding of how trees grow and the weather that brought the limb down. The exploration gives the children ways to develop oral language and academic vocabulary and gives them authentic uses for their budding writing skills.

If Mr. Jay had relied just on pictures of trees, the learning would not have been as rich. Whenever possible, bring nature to your classroom if you do not have opportunities to learn outside. For example, bring in tadpoles and observe how they develop into frogs. Children can use clipboards with paper and pens to record what they see. This will lead to a conversation about the best environment for frogs to live in, so that children develop an understanding that once

the tadpoles turn into frogs, the animals will be returned to their natural habitat. You could bring in a variety of flowers and observe what the different flowers have in common. Then take time to talk about each part of the flower while the children make flower arrangements for the dramatic play center. Plant grass seed in a small paper cup and learn about the necessity for plants to have water and sunlight. Have the children give the grass a trim with scissors. Bring in a variety of seeds and organize them by size. What happens when you plant them? Try planting them in a plastic sandwich bag with a wet paper towel. Tape the bags to the classroom window and watch the roots emerge, along with the stem and leaves. Is there a place where you can transplant your seedlings?

Allowing for active learning using nature indoors often means allowing for messes. If you are teaching in a school that is not open to this, you will need to be creative. This can lead to a discussion on recycling. Asking families for newspapers or old tablecloths to cover tables and floors during messy projects will let families and administrators know that you care about active learning and that you respect the classroom space.

Early Childhood Themes in the Outdoors

Many, if not most, early learning settings use themes to organize their curriculum. If you surveyed a group of early childhood educators to learn the themes they use in their classrooms, you would likely hear themes such as My Community, The Five Senses, and The Four Seasons. The themes ebb and flow year after year. Let's take a look at a few common early childhood themes—pumpkins, firefighters, and colors—and see how you can use the Learning Life Cycle to create authentic, student-driven learning experiences.

PUMPKINS

Walk into any early childhood setting in the United States in October, and you'll probably find pumpkins. Sometimes, children's exposure to pumpkins is limited to uniform cut-out art projects of paper pumpkins stapled to the wall or possibly carving a real pumpkin as a whole-group activity. You can easily transform these lessons into an outdoor classroom of hands-on exploration that includes STEM learning. Here are some ideas to consider for your outdoor learning centers:

➡ Cut off the top of a pumpkin, and encourage the children to scoop out the seeds with their hands (or spoons or other utensils for children who have tactile sensitivities)—there's no need to worry about a mess outside! After this experience, wonder aloud, "Can we eat the seeds that are inside the pumpkin? How would we find out?" Asking these questions is modeling what it is like to wonder and leading your young learners to the next phase of the learning cycle.

→ Set up an outdoor dramatic-play center as a farmer's market so that children can pretend to harvest and sell pumpkins. (See pages 94-100 for easy ways to set up learning centers outside.)

→ Add dried pumpkin seeds to the outdoor math center that children can count or use as money for their farmer's market.

→ Offer children fiction and nonfiction books about pumpkins in an outdoor reading center. (Make sure that the books are protected from the elements if they remain outside.)

→ Add a couple of cut-open pumpkins to the fine-motor and sensory area in the outdoor classroom so that children can feel inside and extract the seeds.

→ In the spring, plant pumpkin seeds in a sunny spot.

In the days after a pumpkin is cut open, children start to witness the process of decomposition. The environmental-education applications are end-less with this project.

Mr. Tom cuts open the pumpkins and puts them in the sensory table for two days so the children can explore. At meeting time, they decide it would be fun to name their pumpkins. Mr. Tom writes the suggestions on a whiteboard. The children take turns voting for their favorite pumpkin name. Afterward, the students discuss where to place the pumpkins outside (grass, sidewalk, field, woods, and so on) and why.

Once they determine the location, the children journal about how their pumpkin looks and return the following week to document any changes in their journals. Questions arise: Are there bugs inside? Why would bugs be inside? Are there any teeth marks? Whose teeth marks could there be? Any mold? How does mold grow? Mr. Tom creates a chart to record children's descriptions of the state of the pumpkins each Monday. They compare how they first described the pumpkins to how they look currently. Students make predictions of what they see and document in their journals what they saw, leading to more conversations about animals in the environment (herbivores, carnivores, and omnivores) that might want to eat the pumpkins. Mr. Tom helps the children answer their questions by providing books and videos on animals and bugs that eat pumpkins, the development of mold, and so on.

Children then share the information in the form of writing a class story, painting pictures, daily journaling of their observations, or making up a song. (Think of the authentic English language arts integration and learning!)

Firefighters

Community helpers is another typical topic in early childhood education. The unit theme of firefighters, like all community helpers, can begin with wonder. What is it like to be a firefighter? Moving this unit outdoors adds a whole new dimension to developing the underlying scientific concepts, as illustrated in the following vignette.

To help children learn what it might be like to be a firefighter, Ms. Emma leads a discussion of what they could use to help them pretend. The children think that squirt bottles would be a good tool to use in their play. Ms Emma notes that using squirt bottles will help with the children's imagination and also build their hand strength for fine-motor skills. Outside, she chooses four children to go with her to the "woods" (a section of trees in their outdoor classroom) to paint "fire" on an old sheet that she has hung on a clothesline. The children then run back to where all the other children are gathered outside and shout, "Fire! Fire! Call 911!" (Other people working at the property were warned that this was a drill.) One child uses a nonworking old phone in the outdoor dramatic play center, which during this time is staged as an outdoor kitchen, to pretend to call 911. Students playing firefighters get the emergency call. They dress quickly in firefighter costumes and grab spray bottles. They run to the woods with their teacher and spray the painted fire until it is out (washed off the sheet). Ms. Emma deconstructs this observable phenomenon and connects it to the science of putting out fires.

The play continues as children take turns being the firefighters, the fire "painters," and calling 911. As they put out the fire, Ms. Emma explains in age-appropriate scientific terms what they are doing. Most of the children use words such as *fuel, ignite,* and *extinguish* in their conversations, building their academic vocabulary in ways that coloring a worksheet of a fire engine does not. In addition, by having the children put on their own firefighting equipment to protect against the "fire" (in

this case, plastic fire helmets to protect from the water bouncing off the fire painted on the sheet), the children get a basic hands-on STEM lesson on how people use tools to solve problems. They learn that firefighters wear special clothes to protect them from fire and heat. Later, they bring the painted sheet inside, and the children continue to reenact the firefighting scenario, this time without water in their squirt bottles.

Ms. Emma explains, "The students participated in every aspect of this activity. I supported their ideas through a play-based activity that came from the research we conducted together." She uses background knowledge and academic vocabulary in daily oral-language lessons, reading aloud books about firefighters, fighting forest fires, and fire safety to the children in their outdoor meeting time. Some of the children shared that they had heard about forest fires on the news. Ms. Emma took this opportunity to ask some "wonder" questions: "What would it be like if we didn't have woods and trees to play in?" "How can we take care of our land so that we don't have a fire?" The discussion led Ms. Emma to set up a visit with firefighters from the local fire department. She asked her young learners what they would like to learn from the firefighters. The children decided they wanted to learn more about their fire truck. They also decided to share their nature journals with the firefighters. The meeting was a collaboration between young learners and professional firefighters, sharing their love of the land.

Colors

Another prevalent topic is colors. In every preschool or learning center, teachers often hear daily conversations about color: "I like the color of your shirt!" "What color is your car?" "What color shoes are you wearing?" Some teachers like the idea of a color of the day, such as "red day," during which everyone wears red and all of the activities are planned around the color red. One creative teacher uses the theme of colors to practice observation skills outside.

Ms. Lilly makes color rings using paint chips from the local hardware store. Each ring has a variety of colors. Ms. Lilly and the children take nature walks and use the color rings to match the colors they find in nature. The children collect pieces of nature (leaves, pine cones, small rocks, acorns) that match the colors in their color rings. They bring their pieces to the outdoor art area and use their collections to make collages and talk more about the colors they see. Building on the discovery of colors in nature, Ms. Lilly decides that she will no longer insist that paint colors at the easels be kept in separate containers. Instead, she stocks the easels with palettes and small amounts of primary-colored paint so that children can mix the paints to get the exact color and shade that they want. By the end of the unit, Ms. Lilly notices that the children are increasing their vocabulary of different colors, learning about mixing colors, and noticing nuances in colors.

By planting experiences, teachers are embracing the inquiry-based teaching approach and naturally turning away from the didactic teacher approach. Children are not fed information in this type of environmental study; instead, they are led to the study and are free to question, hypothesize, observe, document, and test. Young children are natural explorers at the peak of curiosity and need to be led to the information for them to explore and learn about through hands-on investigation. The experiences provided by the teacher make the difference in whether or not an idea can take root, which leads to the next phase of the Learning Life Cycle: growing the roots of wonder.

QUESTIONS FOR REFLECTION AND ACTION

→ Think of a unit of study you recently taught. How can you transform it to be more child driven?

→ How can you bring it outdoors? If you cannot go outside, how can you bring the outdoors in?

→ Have you shared with your students the excitement in finding an answer to a question and applying what you learned? In doing this you are modeling "Aha!" moments.

→ What are you doing in your current practice to leverage the outdoors and STEM education with your themes? How can you shift your current themes to take place outside?

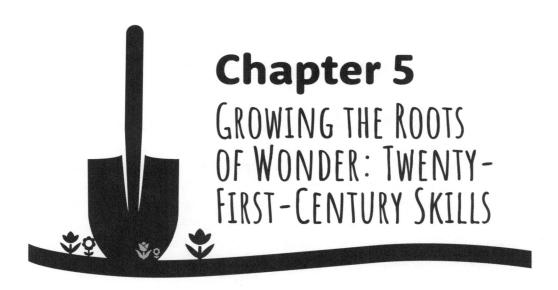

Chapter 5
GROWING THE ROOTS OF WONDER: TWENTY-FIRST-CENTURY SKILLS

Let's take a look at some components of this phase of the learning cycle to better understand how teachers can support children's sense of wonder.

Twenty-First-Century Skills

The great outdoors is a great source of inspiration, and it is the perfect arena for practicing STEM and twenty-first-century skills (Scott, 2017). On the surface, it might seem that outdoor education would only prepare children for an eighteenth-century, pretechnology world. On the contrary, outdoor experiences give all children ample opportunities to solve problems, communicate, create, innovate with tools (the heart of STEM), develop critical-thinking skills, work collaboratively, and master early learning standards in literacy and math—skills that are absolutely necessary to navigate a twenty-first-century world. This foundation leads to citizens who can think critically and use technology strategically. Realizing the change in the work landscape when people who did routine jobs were replaced by computers, researchers saw a need to take a new look at the jobs available and the skills necessary to do those jobs (Jang, 2016). The Partnership for 21st Century Learning, a network of Battelle for Kids (Scott, 2017), developed a collective vision for learning known as *the 21st Century Learning for Early Childhood Framework*. The framework includes skills, knowledge, and expertise that students must master to succeed in work and life, using a blend of content knowledge, specific skills, expertise, and literacies. Our discussion on wonder and curiosity focuses on the learning and innovation skills (also known as the Four Cs) of the framework:

- → Critical thinking
- → Collaboration
- → Creativity
- → Communication (Scott, 2017)

These are the same skills that the U.S. Environmental Protection Agency (EPA) sees as integral to environmental education. Environmental education promotes critical-thinking skills that learners need to make meaningful decisions and even solve problems about their environment. The gift of outdoor education is that wonder naturally happens outdoors. The knowledge that children gain outdoors follows them into adulthood due to the authentic nature of the practice (Bilton, 2018). Children practice critical thinking and learn how to solve real problems while gaining an understanding about their world as they wonder.

Young children are natural explorers and researchers. They are on a quest to understand the environment around them and their place in it. In fact, you can witness the scientific method at work in the way they interact with each new object they encounter (Gurholt and Sanderud, 2016). The following example shows scientific discovery through the eyes of young children:

Picture a group of children playing in the sprinklers on a hot summer day. They

spend hours observing, experimenting, and testing predictions. What makes the water come out of the sprinkler? How high will the water go? Can I control how much water comes out? Is the water cold? What happens when I step on the sprinkler and cover up the holes? What happens to the grass where the sprinkler sits? Each of these questions leads to lessons in science, technology, engineering, and math.

CRITICAL THINKING

There is something about nature that promotes thinking—deep thinking that leads to questioning. This questioning leads to research, research leads to experimenting, and experimenting leads to "Aha!" moments. Outdoor education has a deeper purpose than just providing a place for children to let off steam (Haugen, 2019). Children have the capacity to become "college and career ready," in a developmentally appropriate manner, through outdoor education where they can develop their questioning and problem-solving skills. These critical-thinking skills are the impetus to learning revelations and "Aha!" moments in STEM. For early childhood educators, critical thinking starts with a sense of wonder.

> When was the last time you couldn't wait to share with your students an accomplishment or something you just learned? What do you wonder?

COLLABORATION

Outdoors is also a place where you'll hear, "Look what I found!" or "Watch what happens when I do this!" The outdoors promotes collaboration unlike what you might find within the four walls of a classroom. For example, moving heavy tires, building with large pieces of wood, or climbing tall structures will often be preceded by a call for help from a friend. Activities such as these build physical strength and dexterity. In addition, these experiences build confidence, agency, and self-efficacy: authentic social-emotional learning in action (DeMeulenaere, 2015). SEL is naturally embedded in the outdoor environment and caters to the whole child—physical, social-emotional, intellectual, and spiritual. While some may see these outdoor activities at face value—after all, most of us had recess as part of our school day—we understand that young children learning in outdoor settings are meeting the standards of current educational policy, with the help of their teachers, guides, or mentors.

CREATIVITY

The outdoors is the perfect place to foster curiosity. Today, many families dream that their children will become engineers or scientists. They hope the children will think creatively and then build a spaceship for travel to Mars or will secure a well-paying job as a software engineer who will create the next generation of computer innovation. In this vein, some parents look for early childhood settings for three- and four-year-olds that are regimented and focus on isolated "readiness" skills, such as letter recognition and reading a list of unrelated sight words. However, as we learned from the deep thinkers, the road to innovation is not in rote memorization of facts or, as in Piaget's world, teaching a child a concept before they are ready. Instead, innovation first requires a challenge to overcome, asking questions, and finding solutions to problems. This is the work of the software engineer and other problem solvers. Fostering these skills takes place in environments of discovery, not rote learning. Outdoor settings naturally provide age-appropriate challenges that require creativity and the critical thinking that comes with problem solving. A child might need to find a way to maneuver around play equipment to get to a desired spot to watch a bird, or might want to steady herself on a log to reach a leaf hanging from a branch. The outdoors is a place to foster curiosity, honor the unique strengths children bring to early childhood settings, and give them a place to flourish and use their gifts in ways their teachers had not envisioned.

COMMUNICATION

Communication is a complicated life skill. By listening to others and expressing oneself, a person gains a better understanding of the world. The way teachers ask questions is important in building children's receptive and expressive vocabulary. For example, research shows that when early childhood educators ask open-ended questions during shared book readings, children respond in longer sentences, which often means they are practicing new vocabulary (van der Wilt, van der Veen, and Michaels, 2022).

Educators must also ask closed-ended questions to see whether their students know the answers they are looking for. (Closed-ended questions can be answered with a simple yes or no, or in a few words, and are used to find out facts.) This type of question can be helpful in assessing students' knowledge of core content, such as addition, subtraction, letter and number identification, writing, spelling, and so on. Memorizing facts is necessary in learning these skills. In STEM pedagogy, it's the process in response to open-ended questions that drives our learning. We use the memorized math formulas and reading codes as tools to help make sense of our discovery.

Open-ended questions open up the conversation and have more than one answer. The answers are unique to the individual who is answering. For instance, note the classic open-ended interview question, "What do you see yourself doing five years from now?" Each person will answer that question depending on her own perceptions, ideals, and abilities. Open-ended questions demand reflection on the part of the receiver. They cannot be answered by a simple yes or no. For the early childhood educator, asking open-ended questions is a way to find out what your students already know about a subject. Their answers can then point you to misconceptions that might be part of their understanding about a topic.

Consider, for example, the butterfly release in chapter 2. In considering why the butterflies were not flying out of the open net, there was a strong misconception among the children that butterflies only fly up. The teacher saw this as an opportunity to build on what they did know. She did not correct the misconception; instead, she wondered aloud about another reason for why the butterflies were not flying out, to test the misconception and encourage more learning. If you find it difficult to ask open-ended questions, start by listening to the young learners in your classroom. Get on their level and play. Wonder aloud with them, and you will learn new things about the world as well.

→ I wonder how we can solve this problem.
→ I wonder what it would be like to be a . . . ?
→ I wonder how we can do this together.
→ I wonder what would happen if we . . .
→ I wonder why this happens when I do that.

QUESTIONS FOR REFLECTION AND ACTION

→ Have you shared with your students what you wonder? I wonder why . . . I wonder how . . . I wonder what . . . In this way you are modeling critical thinking for your students.
→ How can children creatively express what they have learned?
→ Can you think of a time when the children in your class were excited to learn something new? What was it like? Was your role more teacher or guide?
→ See appendix A on page 104 for a self-assessment you can use to consider your level of understanding of the Four Cs.

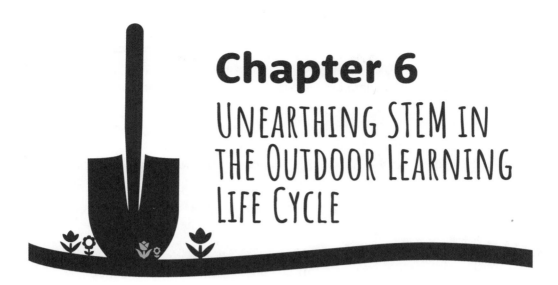

Chapter 6
Unearthing STEM in the Outdoor Learning Life Cycle

A foundation in STEM is increasingly needed to understand the world we live in. Many of us have experienced less than dynamic and relevant science and math lessons that left us asking, "What do I need this for?" No matter what our experience or background in STEM, it is up to early childhood educators to open that world to their students. This often means finding the joy, spark, or wonder for ourselves as teachers so we can share that wonder with our students. Science, technology, engineering, and math are the tools needed to unearth the joy of discovery.

This chapter begins with a discussion of STEM and how it is an integral part of the Learning Life Cycle. We will then give you two examples of STEM lessons, one initiated by a child, the other by a teacher.

Science, Technology, Engineering, and Math = STEM

The acronym STEM did not come into common usage until the early 2000s, when the technology revolution of personal computers and smartphones created a renewed focus on STEM. In the first decade of the twenty-first century, most states developed STEM standards of practice for their pre-K–12 students, as some felt the United States was slipping "behind" internationally (McClure et al., 2017). Most jobs today demand competence with STEM. The STEM subjects are not just about memorizing math facts or the scientific and engineering practices. Students need to see how STEM skills help them make discoveries and think critically about real life. This takes guidance from a teacher who is excited to learn with his students. As we have learned in the second stage of the Learning Life Cycle, children naturally have many questions about the outdoor environment, particularly their own environment. Whether it be on a walk from home to the bus, playing in a public space, or exploring in one's own backyard, children will notice the smallest shifts in weather and nuances and changes in trees, rocks, and dirt on the ground. This natural curiosity lends itself to discovery, which is at the heart of STEM.

STEAM

Add the arts and you have STEAM! In 2013, John Maeda, former president of Rhode Island School of Art and Design, was the first champion of adding the arts to STEM (Burry, 2018). His rationale was that, to solve problems effectively, the context needs to be considered. A foundation in the arts provides this context. Looking back at our deep thinkers and how Montessori equated children's play to poetry, it is no wonder that learning through the arts gives STEM context.

SCIENCE

The sciences cover a diverse and expansive knowledge base, including the following disciplines:

- **Physical sciences:** physics, chemistry, astronomy, and so on
- **Earth sciences:** geology, meteorology, geography, oceanography, and so on
- **Life sciences:** biology, physiology, botany, zoology, and so on

It can be helpful to realize that with so many options, there are many opportunities to use science to find answers. While teachers do not need to have a comprehensive knowledge in the sciences, they do need to have a sense of wonder to follow the scientific method with their students and to learn alongside them when the teachers do not have expertise in a certain discipline. Teachers must be willing to embrace the experimental part of science that may not reveal the answers they expect. In Malaguzzi's words, a teacher must "relish uncertainty" in the science disciplines.

Also necessary is a practice of scaffolding for students so that they get from one level of understanding to the next. A teacher who listens to his students will find some common interests and can use these to build his plan. He can lead children to discovery as scientists do, using the scientific method. The four phases of the Learning Life Cycle are represented in the steps of the scientific method.

The Scientific Method and the Learning Life Cycle

Scientific Method	Corresponding Phase of the Learning Life Cycle
Ask a question.	Experience leads to wonder
Do background research.	Growing the roots of wonder
Construct a hypothesis.	STEM
Test the hypothesis.	STEM
Analyze the results.	STEM
Share the data.	Creative expression, communication

TECHNOLOGY

STEM is the scientific method, finding and then solving problems. The *T* in STEM is for technology tools used to solve problems. The most complex computer is not the *T* in STEM unless it is used to solve a problem. For example, in an early childhood classroom, children may be at a center watching a video on a tablet. In this case, the tablet is not considered the *T* in STEM because it is not solving a problem; it is just a device to watch a video. However, if that same tablet is used to take pictures of an investigation the children are doing on how a pumpkin decomposes so they can go back and analyze this data, that use is the *T* in STEM. For young children and their adult scientist counterparts, technology can be a magnifying glass to see the detail of a butterfly wing or a pair of tweezers to get a sliver out of a finger.

ENGINEERING

The *E* in STEM stands for engineering. The primary job of an engineer of any kind—aerospace, mechanical, civil, electrical, software—is to solve problems. The process by which they solve problems is the engineering design process. First, they ask questions: What is the problem? What needs to be solved? Next, they conduct research on how to solve the problem and imagine different ways they might apply what they have learned to this problem. With this information, they construct a prototype of a solution and test it to see if it does solve the problem. Evaluation comes next: Was the problem solved? Why or why not? The prototype is then reconstructed based on the findings and tested again. This process continues until the engineers are satisfied that the problem has been solved.

In the world of children in outdoor settings, engineering can take the form of collecting rainwater to water the garden during dry spells or building a bridge over a child-made "river" using natural materials and loose parts. Engineering is actually a part of all of our lives as we navigate and solve problems. An outdoor learning space is a place where authentic problems occur naturally; here, children as engineers can use their tools to solve them.

MATH

Finally, the *M* in STEM is math. Math is used as a tool to understand the world and assist in solving problems. Many states are currently using standards based on the Common Core State Standards (CCSS) developed in conjunction with the National Governors Association and business leaders (2010). The main focus of these standards is not on rote memorization of math facts but on the ability to use computational skills to solve problems. A few of the big-picture goals for math in the CCSS are making sense of problems and solving them, reasoning abstractly and quantitatively, constructing viable arguments and critiquing the reasoning of others, and using appropriate tools strategically and with precision. Outdoor learning is where these big-picture goals happen naturally and

authentically. Children need to master counting and computation; however, if the learning stops there and is not applied to problem solving, then they will not be able to use the skills they have learned. It is interesting to note that the first overall goal includes perseverance. All the capability to do math does not matter if a person does not have the perseverance to stay with a task until it is completed. Outdoor learning provides the environment necessary to discover or create problems that are worth solving and worthy of the perseverance and effort needed to do so.

In the following example, we see an outdoor learning opportunity in action. As you read, look for the elements of STEM in action.

A Child-Initiated Outdoor STEM Lesson

For teachers to develop a child-initiated theme, they need to first discover what children get excited about. The easiest way to do this is to pay attention to their play.

One afternoon on the playground, students begin to dig in the dirt. The teacher notices that the children are completely immersed in their play. He and his coteacher decide to forgo the lesson plan for the day and encourage the children to continue their play.

One student finds a worm, and the other students immediately come over to look. The children ask questions:

- How does it feel when you touch it?
- Where is its head? Does it have eyes?
- What's that band on it?
- Where did you dig to find it?
- Why are they on our playground?

The excitement of holding a live creature stirs up a natural curiosity that the teachers can't ignore. They decide to use these questions—signs that wonder (the second phase in the Learning Life Cycle) is taking place—to make up the environmental education theme of worms.

Teachers might hesitate to try this approach, especially if they know little about the topic. However, teachers who take the time to research a topic with their students find it to be an enriching experience for everyone. Research is not difficult. Strategic searches on the internet will yield the information needed to explain scientific concepts to young children and their families. (See appendix C on page 109 for a list of resources.)

One of the first questions the children asked their teachers when it was time to go inside was whether they could bring the worms into their classroom. To promote student agency, teachers decided to support the children in researching whether it was a good idea to bring the worms inside. They provided nonfiction and fiction books from the library so that students had access to the information in their book center. In one of their nonfiction books, they found out about wormeries, which led them to the next project: their own classroom wormery.

The teachers provide an old aquarium to make the wormery. The students help engineer it by adding newspaper bedding, dirt, compost, and of course, worms they find on the playground. They place the wormery at eye level so that everyone can see it, and the teachers challenge the students by asking questions such as,

- What do worms need in the wormery to live?
- How many worms should we put in the wormery?
- How can we make the wormery dark in our classroom when the lights are on? What tools will we need?
- What should the worms eat?

The students begin to learn about what worms do (they make, irrigate, and aerate soil) and their importance to our environment. Using the wormery, the same experiments that Charles Darwin conducted are done in the classroom. The students make predictions, journal about their hypotheses (with scaffolding from their teachers), and use the scientific method to determine whether a particular hypothesis is true.

- Which leaves will worms prefer—celery or carrot? (These worms prefer celery leaves.)
- What happens when a loud noise vibrates through the wormery? (Worms will tunnel down to avoid predators.)

In the example above, the teachers were confident that all this research and conversation using the scientific method would lead to learning about STEM. There are many ways that teachers can incorporate worms into every center of their outdoor or indoor classroom. For example, dramatic play can include "worm" scientists using microscopes. The table work can have worm specimens that children examine and use as an example to draw and label. For writing activities that take place outside, children are given notebooks or clipboards to provide a stable place to write. Students can build the life cycle of a worm with loose parts. The art easel can be used to paint the wormery or the worms on the playground. Teachers don't have to provide "worm colored" paint but rather let children mix paints to find the right color for the worm; or instead of paint, children can collect dirt, add water, and paint with mud. Journals can be used to document the experiments. Rulers can be used to measure worms and a chart can be kept in the room documenting the lengths of worms. These can be ordered from shortest to longest.

All of the disciplines are covered through the student-initiated theme lens of worms. Students are learning math when they are measuring and digging to certain depths. They are learning literacy through the books that are both available and read to them. They are learning about environmental science through the wormery. Language arts is learned through recording findings in journals. Social studies is learned through jobs surrounding worms, such as scientists and farmers. Technology use is evident by the tools used for digging, writing, painting, measuring, and recording via tablets.

Ultimately, perhaps the most important lesson that the children learned was that the worms seemed healthier outside. Inside their wormery, the environment wasn't quite right, and many of the worms didn't survive. The children decided that worms are happier outdoors.

The children's experiences outside led to wondering about worms, which led to using STEM to find answers, which led to new knowledge and sharing ideas. What will these new ideas lead to next? The Outdoor Learning Life Cycle will surely repeat itself, as the outdoors will offer new experiences as the seasons change.

Transforming a Teacher-led STEM Activity

Next, let's look at how transforming a lesson for outside learning can change a typical teacher-led activity in the classroom into a child-driven learning experience. To do this, the teacher will shift his way of thinking about the lesson and how the children will participate. The teacher's new ways of thinking will evolve into the creation of a child-driven outdoor cooking unit. First, let's start with the teacher's original cooking lesson.

A preschool teacher plans a cooking project—baking a cake—to show how math is used in the kitchen. He sits at the center of a table in the classroom, and the young learners sit where they can watch but not touch. The teacher allows the children to take turns stirring the batter, with only a few seconds of swipes around the bowl per child. The actual time they come in contact with any of the ingredients or utensils is minimal. The teacher measures and pours, mixes ingredients, and then cleans up the table while a teacher's helper takes the cake to an oven to bake.

While the ingredients are real, the teacher-led activity leaves little room for authentic work on the part of the learner and no opportunity to learn through the discovery of exploring mistakes (McLeod and Shareski, 2018). The indoor classroom cooking unit involves tightly restrained parameters developed by the teacher to stay in control (McLeod and Shareski, 2018). There are few surprises, other than an occasional mishap such as spilling water or forgetting to add salt. Often, mishaps like these are not seen as learning experiences but more as negative interferences.

Compliance and conformity were the goals in the teacher-led lesson (McLeod and Shareski, 2018). In this scenario, the teacher could have been easily replaced by a cooking show found on the internet. Now let's focus on steps teachers can take to move away from an indoor, teacher-led cooking activity to an outdoor, child-driven activity.

Shifting Perspective

Would the children in the first scenario learn that math is used in the kitchen? Yes. But what is the importance of that knowledge, and how will they use it in the future? The goals of that lesson were limited. What was meant as a math activity was in reality a lesson on practicing listening skills—and a frustrating one at that. Instead of passive participants, the students need to be active learners. The teacher will need to focus on the developmentally appropriate skills he would like his students to practice. Deeper learning can happen if students are allowed to wrestle and play with the content (McLeod and Graber, 2019; McLeod and Shareski, 2018). This approach will allow for creativity for both the teacher and the students. Questions that provoke critical thinking are the foundation for a tool called the 4 Shifts Protocol, which can be used to consider how to transform a unit for deeper learning (McLeod and Shareski, 2018). The 4 Shifts Protocol focuses on

deeper thinking, authentic work, student agency and personalization, and technology infusion (McLeod and Shareski, 2018). Scott McLeod and Julie Graber (2019) developed this tool to help educators integrate technology in their programs for deeper learning experiences. The tool is valuable for teachers and administrators who want to redesign lessons and themes. We like it as a tool for making the subtle shifts necessary for deeper outdoor learning and have made some additions to meet that goal. You can access the original 4 Shifts Protocol online. (https://docs.google.com/document/d/1COUR5p1E1gi-r8Hk0WXfYwzVX3Fw6fSNdvHvggVBJMc/edit) McLeod and Graber suggest that teachers begin with considering the goals of the lesson and ways to incorporate critical thinking, reflection, authenticity, and creativity.

Begin by selecting a lesson to work on. Choose one or more of the four shifts (deeper thinking, authentic work, student agency and personalization, and technology infusion) and examine your current practice to consider ways to enhance the lesson.

→ **Deeper Thinking and Learning**
- Domain knowledge: What curriculum standards will my students be meeting?

- Critical thinking: What open-ended questions will I ask?

- Problem solving: Is there a problem that needs solving? How will I integrate STEM to solve the problem?

- Creativity: Do students have an opportunity to express their knowledge in ways that are personal to them?

- Metacognition: Am I making room in the lesson for students to reflect on the work (with teacher guidance) so that they can express what they have learned?

- Assessment alignment: How will I incorporate the children in assessing the learning that takes place?

→ **Authentic Work**
- Real or fake? Is my lesson pertaining to real people, animals, or the environment that my students might experience outside of school?

- Authentic role: Are my students practicing roles in an authentic way?

- Domain practices: Are my students practicing vocabulary specific to the discipline, such as *equation* in math or "a butterfly eats with its *proboscis*" in science?

- **Authentic tools:** Are my students using tools that are authentic to the lesson?

- **Authentic assessment:** Will my assessment incorporate developmentally appropriate practice and authentically represent what each child can do?

→ **Student Agency and Personalization**
  - Who selects the learning goals?

  - Who selects the activities?

  - Who selects how students will demonstrate their knowledge?

  - Who is the primary driver of talk time/work time?

  - Whose interests are represented?

  - Who selects the technology?

→ **Technology Infusion**
  - How are students communicating? in pairs? in groups larger than three? alone with the teacher?

  - Is technology used to facilitate communication? photos? writing? charts/graphs?

  - Is there collaboration with students in class? with students in other classes? with students at other schools? with families?

Let's think about the indoor cooking lesson. Two shifts that could transform this lesson are authentic work and student agency. To check for authenticity, consider whether the students' work is authentic and reflective of the work that is done by experts (McLeod and Graber, 2019). In this case, the students are passively listening and watching. They were not using discipline-specific practices and processes of real cooks and chefs, such as measuring, mixing, and reading or writing a recipe. Next, let's consider student agency. The lesson is controlled by the teacher. She selected the learning goals and activity, drives the talk and work time, and chooses and uses the technology (McLeod and Graber, 2019). The teacher is the "sage on the stage," an approach that is not effective in reaching deeper learning outcomes. The task of watching the teacher cook is undemanding and tedious, especially if each child has to wait for a turn to stir the batter for only a few seconds. Deeper learning competencies of thinking critically and working collaboratively are not happening (Hewlett Foundation,

2013). By asking students to watch and not touch, the teacher is unwittingly squelching opportunities for them to think critically or solve complex problems. They aren't being encouraged to work collaboratively with their peers or even use the authentic tools and technology (hand mixer, spoons, spatulas) required for the project.

To provide opportunities for deeper learning, the teacher needs a place where children could practice cooking skills without the worry of mistakes or messes. From this point of view, designing a cooking lesson around an outdoor kitchen makes sense. The teacher decides that the purpose of the cooking unit is to have the students actually practice pouring water, measuring and mixing ingredients, writing recipes, and sequencing. The activity becomes more innovative simply by redesigning the lesson to meet these goals. Even though the ingredients in an outdoor kitchen will not be edible, the authenticity will be found in the hands-on nature of the children's work.

Teachers in schools that have outdoor kitchens report that children have more control, power, and independence, signs that student agency is present in their programs (McLeod and Shareski, 2018; Natural Start, 2013). In the outdoor kitchen environment, children also have a better understanding of math concepts such as *conservation*—the understanding that the quantity of something stays the same even though the appearance changes (for example, twelve counting bears are still twelve in number, whether they are bunched together in a shorter line or spread out in a longer line). This is Piaget in action.

> . . . there is evidence that kids can make rapid breakthroughs if we simply let them do the pouring and rolling. When 105 first graders participated in a series of seven conservation tasks—involving water, clay, coins, and string—children randomly assigned to carry out "hands-on" demonstrations outperformed kids who merely observed them. On every task, the active learners were more likely to show a grasp of the conservation principle, and the difference was particularly striking among the kids who struggled the most. About 30% of the passive observers didn't seem to understand conservation during any of the tasks. By contrast, only 4% of active learners showed this level of confusion. Hands-on activities appear to have made a crucial difference (Dewar, 2016).

Another benefit of moving lessons outdoors is that it helps teachers avoid lessons that involve passive observation. Dewar (2016) says, "Kids don't need to wait in line to touch a leaf or feel the smooth contours of a stone." The entire outdoor area is literally their classroom.

Incorporating Student Agency

In rethinking the cooking lesson, the teacher makes setting up the outdoor kitchen part of the curriculum. He involves the children by wondering aloud, "I wonder where the best place would be to set up an outdoor kitchen," and "I wonder what kind of utensils we will need" (Tinkergarten, 2019). These types of prompts give children context and a starting point that will foster imagination and excitement, much like the obstacle course mentioned in chapter 2. Young children's imaginations can turn logs into stoves and trees into refrigerators. Once the group agrees on the parameters, children create labels in the writing center to be posted as reminders. They designate outdoor furniture as the stove and work area of the outdoor kitchen. They use a simple table with a shelf underneath to hold pots and pans.

Making an Outdoor Kitchen

You can get your community involved by asking for donations to build your outdoor kitchen. Design your kitchen with the following in mind:

- Do you have a water source? Is there a faucet available? Is there another way to bring water to the space?

- What materials does the site offer? For example, does it have dirt, acorns, sticks, mulch, and so on? What will need to be added?

- What furniture is available? For example, is there a picnic table? Could the children utilize plastic cartons or wooden boxes?

- What tools will the children need? For example, do you want them to experience using measuring cups and spoons; using large spoons, whisks, egg beaters, and pastry blender for stirring and mixing; implementing bowls of all sizes and pots and pans?

- What materials and tools could be donated by families or purchased from thrift shops? For example, could families donate a tortilla press, a wok, chopsticks, or a mortar and pestle? oven mitts? plastic plates?

Developing Project Goals

When setting up your outdoor kitchen, develop goals for the project. For example, by working with the outdoor kitchen, learners will display student agency by creating their own recipes, collaborating with their peers, and presenting their ideas to their teachers and families. They will participate in authentic learning experiences by using real kitchen utensils, pouring water, and measuring ingredients. They will learn and practice skills that support STEM subjects. They will display increased knowledge about people in the culinary-arts profession in their dramatic play.

Aligning to Standards

The outdoor kitchen lesson plan that the preschool teacher created draws on relevant standards (see the following) for students from the International Society for Technology in Education (ISTE). ISTE has developed standards to help teachers empower student voices and ensure that learning is a student-driven process (ISTE, n.d.). Alternatively, you may choose to use the standards and frameworks for prekindergarten from your own state or school district.

ISTE Standards

➡ **Standard 3.** Knowledge Constructor
  - Students build knowledge by actively exploring real-world issues and problems, developing ideas and theories, and pursuing answers and solutions.

➡ **Standard 4.** Innovative Designer
  - Students develop, test, and refine prototypes as part of a cyclical design process.

  - Students exhibit a tolerance for ambiguity, perseverance, and the capacity to work with open-ended problems.

➡ **Standard 6.** Creative Communicator
  - Students choose the appropriate platforms and tools for meeting the desired objectives of their creation or communication. (ISTE, n.d.)

As an example, if the school is located in Maryland, the teacher might align the transformed cooking lesson to that state's pre-K standards:

➡ **Writing:** Use a combination of drawing, dictating, or developmentally appropriate writing to state information on a topic.
➡ **Language:** Identify real-life connections between words and their use.

→ **Math:**
  - Describe measurable attributes of objects, such as length or weight.

  - Explore relationships by comparing groups of objects up to five and then up to ten.

  - Identify whether the number of objects in one group is greater than, less than, or equal to the number of objects in another group (e.g., by using matching and counting strategies).

Taking the technology outside and allowing the young learners to manipulate them significantly modifies the original cooking lesson. The students have access to experimentation, which was stifled by the original teacher-led instruction. New tasks redefine the lesson, including creating recipes and learning about the various jobs in a restaurant kitchen. Redefining the important aspects of the cooking lesson ultimately leads to student-led, innovative learning. Students in the outdoor kitchen will master core academic content by learning new vocabulary typically used in restaurant kitchens as well as develop fine-motor skills while practicing measuring, pouring, and stirring dirt, acorns, and twigs. They will collaborate by taking turns playing the different roles of executive chef, chef de cuisine, sous-chef, station chef, pastry chef, dishwasher, customer, and wait staff (Collier, 2018). They will learn to communicate effectively, developing and recording recipes. Finally, with teacher scaffolding (think Vygotsky in chapter 3), they will reflect on their work and develop a more academic mindset shown by the ability to change course or tactics to obtain their goal.

It is important to offer outdoor experiences, no matter how limited, so that children and teachers can begin to see these positive changes in their programs and then build on their successes.

Questions for Reflection and Action

→ As a teacher, what do you choose first when planning a lesson: the activity or the standards? Why?

→ What can you do to redesign lessons for outdoor learning to create deeper learning opportunities?

→ How does moving a lesson outdoors change the way you address the standards?

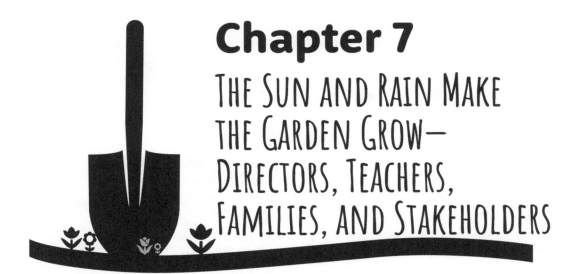

Chapter 7
The Sun and Rain Make the Garden Grow— Directors, Teachers, Families, and Stakeholders

The key to an effective outdoor education program for young children is stakeholders who have the conceptual understanding of how young children learn, how current policy drives instruction, and how STEM-infused outdoor education works in the context of young children. Perhaps you have been thinking about adding an outdoor classroom but you don't know where to start. Will your staff be on board with this new idea? How about the families? the community? The most important thing to remember is that it will take time and patience to start something new, even if that something is awesome and obviously beneficial to children.

This chapter provides the strategies necessary to get started thinking and acting on how to implement STEM-infused outdoor experiences for your students. These strategies are framed in the experience of one administrator who quickly pivoted when the global pandemic hit in 2020 to re-create her indoor preschool as an outdoor one.

Administrators: Gardeners with Green Thumbs

Have you ever visited a friend's garden and seen that everything is blooming at just the right time? The saying goes that this person must have a "green thumb," meaning everything they touch grows. Of course, this negates the true reasons the garden is blooming. The gardener has studied how to create the best soil conditions, which plants will grow in that specific environment, how much water is needed, whether the plant needs sun or shade, what to do about plant diseases, how to know if the plant is sick, which plants look good next to each other, and so on.

A gardener's job is similar to the job of the administrator. The best administrators are leaders who make leading look easy. Their schools are known for their quality educational opportunities. Their teachers seem happy to be at work. They seem to be on the cutting edge of all best practices. However, we know that there is no magic—or green thumb—in being a good administrator.

Good administrators have a desire to stay relevant in a changing world. Their role requires a commitment to sound theory and practice and a willingness to practice the twenty-first-century learning skills of collaboration, critical thinking, creative expression, and communication. In short, it takes a lot of work! The following vignette shows the journey of one administrator's outdoor classroom start-up.

The COVID-19 pandemic forced preschools to rethink how to deliver quality care for the children and families they serve. Maggie, the director of a church preschool, worked with her team, her board of directors, and other stakeholders to figure out how to navigate safely reopening their preschool. Maggie had long known the benefits of outdoor learning and was pleased to learn that the virus does not spread as easily outside as it does indoors. She found that this was one reason that other schools were starting outdoor programs. She suggested to the stakeholders that they should study how to offer an outdoor preschool option as a way to keep the school open and meet the needs of children and families. The board agreed that the approach was worth considering and recommended creating an outdoor-education task force to investigate the possibilities. The task force consisted of Maggie, a few of the board members, three teachers from the preschool, a professor of early childhood education from a local university, and a member of the congregation with a passion for nature who had implemented a previous project installing a rain garden on the property. For their first meeting, Maggie invited a guest director who shared her photos of a trip she had taken to Sweden to visit the forest schools there. (Forest schools are outdoor schools prevalent in that area of the world.) The task force heard for the first time the philosophy, "There is no bad weather, just bad clothing!" This started a spirited conversation about just how much they can embrace the outdoor-school philosophy. It was quite a leap for some of the members to consider a full-time outdoor preschool, but the idea of being outside for part of the day seemed reasonable.

Maggie did more research on outdoor learning and found a preschool with an outdoor classroom within an hour of their school. She arranged for the task force to tour the classroom. This pivotal, hands-on experience solidified the idea of creating their own outdoor classroom. In particular, the task force members noticed that the STEM learning that had already been incorporated in their program could be enriched through outdoor experiences. In a subsequent meeting with the board of directors, the outdoor-education task force shared pictures of the outdoor classroom. Their excitement was

contagious: the board agreed that an outdoor classroom was a good idea. As the site for the new classroom, the pastor recommended a beautiful wooded area on the property that was not in use.

Whenever starting a new addition to a child-care space, administrators need to consider licensing and zoning issues. The outdoor classroom was no exception. The school's rain garden had not needed additional zoning permission, but the outdoor classroom required a "change of use" permit. Their nature-enthusiast rain-garden-installer member agreed to tackle the zoning issue.

There was one glitch in the whole operation: the absence of a fence. Maggie knew that, to safely care for children in the outdoor classroom, there would need to be a fence, but fences are expensive, especially on a limited budget. With the help of a member of the outdoor-education task force, Maggie applied for four grants, and two were accepted. The fence project would be completed once the zoning application was approved several months later.

Early Childhood Teachers: The Sun and the Rain

Teachers come to the profession with their own experiences and biases. Many choose early childhood because of their inclination to be nurturers. Like the sun and the rain, early childhood educators nurture the experiences they've planted, allowing questions to take root, and supporting learning through STEM and creative expression. However beautiful this analogy is, not all teachers may feel confident teaching STEM outdoors (Barrable and Lakin, 2020). That's okay. The best way to introduce teachers to outdoor learning is through hands-on experiences of their own. Professional development in an outdoor setting can bring about conversations regarding weather, appropriateness of activities, fear of the environment, and more.

While the task force waited for approval of their zoning application, Maggie wanted to share the outdoor classroom experience with the rest of her staff. She arranged for a training at the nature-based learning center that had inspired the task force. She also reached out to families at the preschool and offered a few seats to interested families. On a walk one afternoon before the training, she noticed a neighbor taking pictures of birds and invited her to the training as well. Together, the community of caregivers and interested parties learned about the possibilities of outdoor education through hands-on experiences, toured the learning-center's outdoor classroom, and hiked to the nearby meadow. The weather was cold in the morning, delightful by 11:00 a.m., and pouring rain at 2:00 p.m. What an authentic way to experience outdoor learning! The teachers started to embrace the concepts, and back at the preschool, they allowed their students to spend more time on the playground and even took them for nature hikes. One day of training was enough to inspire the teachers to start planting the seeds of new outdoor experiences.

As Maggie found, some families also desire these opportunities. Allowing teachers and families to express their feelings, while offering scaffolding to support their learning and readiness to teach outside can make a huge difference. All learners, even families and teachers, need authentic experiences to help them understand concepts. Having access to an outdoor classroom and observing teachers and children who thrive in that setting is priceless professional development.

In addition to authentic learning experiences, teachers can take the self-assessment at the end of this chapter to bring to light their own feelings about outdoor education. Challenging as it may be, teachers can rise above current attitudes if they can recognize the roadblocks. Are they willing to take risks? Are they sensitive to the interests of the children? What opportunities are they missing because of a desire to keep clean instead of green? What do they wonder about their environment? What part of their world and experiences with the environment are they willing to share with children? The following chart lists common fears that teachers may have and offers ways for teachers to reframe those fears so that they can move forward.

Stuck in the Muck: Valid Fears and How to Reframe Them

Fears	Challenge Thoughts
Fear of someone getting hurt	I will make sure the area is clear of obvious dangers. I am up to date on my first-aid training. I am also good at supervision.
Fear of getting dirty	I can wash my hands at work, and I can shower or bathe when I return home. I can wear clothes that are okay to get dirty.
Fear of living things, such as insects, snakes, poison ivy/oak, and so on	I can learn about living things in the environment and develop a healthy respect for all living things.
Fear of not being able to cover core STEM learning content	I understand that to give the core STEM concepts meaning, children must have access to interesting experiences. Outdoor experiences lead to STEM!

Fear of working with other teachers who have negative attitudes about the outdoor environment	I understand that everyone has fears and that those fears may be influencing negative behavior.
Fear of asking permission from the administrator to take the class outside	I can show my excitement about outdoor education and present plans that show how outdoor learning would support a specific STEM project.
Fear of the weather	I have access to shelter in case of extreme weather conditions. I have clothes and shoes that support being outdoors in different types of weather.
Fear of family pushback	I can educate families on the benefits of outdoor learning and, if necessary, gradually add outdoor activities until they see the joy and learning these activities bring to their young children.

If you can relate to any of these fears, you are not alone. It takes time to confront fears that may be keeping you from truly experiencing the joy of outdoor learning, especially for those with no prior experience playing in nature. A good way to start is to be your own nurturer and provide yourself with some outdoor experiences. Ask a friend to go with you on a short hike at your local park. Start small and see where that experience takes you. Incremental change is good. Even if you cannot have a complete outdoor education center, any small steps you take to that end will benefit your students. Often the most challenging part of starting is getting used to taking risks. In early childhood settings there is often a hyperfocus on keeping children safe, as there should be. However, the next section will assist teachers in creating spaces for appropriate risk-taking.

Risk-Taking with Limit Setting and Structure

The positive changes adults observe when children are outdoors do not mean the need for limit setting and structure disappears. However, outdoor learning requires a different type of limit setting. The value of learning outdoors is great enough that some risk is worth it. In explaining the value, Friedrich Froebel (the inventor of kindergarten) gave the example of a child climbing a tree, "To climb a new tree is to discover a new world; . . . we should not be so insensitive to call out, 'Come down you will fall'" (Tovey, 2017). John Dewey saw problems as learning opportunities: "We only think when we are confronted with problems," and "Failure is instructive. The person who really thinks learns quite as much from his failures as from his successes" (Smith, 2021).

These words ring true in early childhood settings. Educators need to set up instruction so children can solve problems and learn from the process and outcomes of their discovery (Johnson and Reed, 2012). Instead of setting seemingly arbitrary rules and procedures, outdoor learning leads to collaborative parameters based on logical consequences. Gurholt and Sanderud (2016) illustrate that curious play is a valid alternative to the concept of risky play by focusing on what motivates children's play in nature. They contend that children are motivated by curiosity: "Rather than seeking risk for its own sake, they accept it as part of their continual search for new affordances that will enable them to discover and create new knowledge of themselves and the world they inhabit" (Gurholt and Sanderud, 2016). Risk-taking is a necessary component of outdoor learning, and critical thinking is encouraged so children learn what risks are appropriate and what should be avoided. For instance, after a rainy day, a teacher might wonder aloud, "I wonder if the log will be too slippery to climb because it is wet," or "Do you feel stable on that rock?" Teachers can also set physical boundaries by tying fabric to a tree that children are not to climb on and giving children landmarks on where to race to. While on a nature walk, teachers can point out blazes (trail markers painted on trees) that show the path to follow. When it is time to regather, a teacher can yell a particular bird call or animal sound that the class decides on ahead of time.

Addressing Family Concerns

The task force was convinced an outdoor program would serve their community in exciting ways; however, there was concern that some families wanted what they believed to be a more academic approach to outdoor learning (that is to say, children sitting at desks quietly filling out worksheets) instead of the play-based methods the teachers were planning to use. To address their concerns, the task force held an open house in the new space to explain the learning that takes place outdoors and to allow parents to ask questions. The teachers set up the outdoor classroom with magnifying glasses, field guides, and paper and crayons to make bark rubbings. The teachers interacted with the children as they would on a typical preschool day, opening up conversations by asking questions such as, "How does the bark feel? What kinds of bugs will we find on this log? Show me how you can balance on this stepping stone!" The teachers explicitly explained to the parents how these learning activities connected to the learning standards and the assessments associated with them for "school readiness." The parents responded favorably to their children playing in nature. In fact, some parents took pictures to share with other family members and friends. The open house also provided a tour of the school building, where the teachers had

various nature activities for the children to interact with, such as using a stick to write the first letter of their name in wet sand. The children also categorized stones of different sizes and shapes and made forsythia paintings with yellow and brown paint. Again, the teachers explicitly showed the families how these activities connected to literacy and math learning as well as critical thinking. Families got a taste of how nature was infused in all parts of the program and saw that their children were learning while having fun.

Some families will not need any prodding to sign their child up for a nature-based program. Those families most likely have happy memories of playing outdoors as children. Others may be interested in a nature-based program because of the way it can complement STEM learning.

The families at Maggie's preschool had conflicting views and expected more guided STEM lessons in the outdoor setting. It is important to know that some concepts, such as scientific observation skills, are better understood when a teacher acts as a guide to show the steps involved in learning (Yurumezoglu and Cin, 2019). A teacher who guides young learners in creating a game or shows them the steps involved in observing ants and then researching about their homes is scaffolding students' learning so that they can build on what they know. These interactions need to take place for rich learning experiences to occur.

Recent research about teachers' and families' perspectives at an outdoor preschool shows that teachers who embrace outdoor learning see their roles as observers (Hunter, Graves, and Bodensteiner, 2017). Families want to see teachers involved in their children's learning, not mere observers of their learning. To know when to observe and when to guide is a skill that takes practice. However, if teachers explicitly explain their teaching methods to families, both at family-education opportunities and in weekly communications, then families will understand how this type of learning supports critical thinking and the acquisition of literacy and math skills.

To help families learn with you and their children about environmental education, communicate often about what the children are doing and learning, for example: "Today we observed ants building a nest and noticed them carrying food. We read a book about ants and learned that a group of ants is called a *colony*. We also learned that the ants that leave the nest to look for food are called *foragers*. Then we played a game pretending we were foragers looking for food to bring back to our nest. We pretended the acorns were ant food and counted how many we collected." Families with young children, just like teachers, have various comfort levels with nature.

Teachers and administrators can post nature resources in the community that would be appropriate for young families to explore on the weekend. Schools can make room to have family volunteers accompany them on nature walks.

With the natural deterioration of materials that takes place outdoors, a wish list can be an ongoing way to ask for family help in replacing old logs or spreading new mulch. Tap into families' strengths and allow them to have those "Aha!" moments, too!

As with all relationship building, communication is key. In Maggie's experience, one of the parents, upon first hearing about outdoor education, strongly opposed the idea. Maggie kept an open attitude toward this parent and continued to share resources about the benefits of outdoor education. After a few months, the parent saw the benefits on the face of her happy child when she came home every day filled with stories of what she had learned that day. This parent became the number-one supporter of the school. She took it upon herself to have a fundraiser to buy a class set of insulated rain boots and dropped by one day with a box of sedimentary rocks she had found in her backyard. An open mind, family education, and happy, learning children will change the minds of most families if they are hesitant.

The practical aspect of outdoor learning includes choosing clothing that is designed for play. Children and staff need to have coats that will keep them warm in cold weather, boots for rainy and muddy terrain, hats, mittens, sunscreen, and bug spray. It is best to inform families before they enroll their child that these are the expectations. Families will need guidance as to what is necessary for your particular climate. Additional resources can be found in appendix C on page 109.

Requiring families to purchase their own outdoor gear presents a problem for those with limited resources. Some schools start a clothing exchange each year so that they can pass down coats or boots that have been outgrown to other younger children entering the program. Others have recruited sponsors from their community to purchase gear for families who cannot afford it. With creativity and tenacity, schools can make sure that everyone who wants to come out and play can participate.

Working with the Community

The surprising outcome for Maggie was the interest that the community developed for the outdoor-classroom project. To obtain the correct county zoning, several community meetings were required, which gave the task force an opportunity to present its vision. The neighborhood was happy that the land would be used in its natural state. The director created a presentation that explained the goal of the outdoor classroom, which was used on several different occasions to the church council, county zoning, and parent community. As a result, the various community groups were receiving a unified message about the purpose of the outdoor classroom.

One member of the church built a sizable outdoor kitchen using repurposed lumber. Several church members organized mulch-spreading parties. The woodworking club of the nearby retirement village created signs, and a Boy Scout built child-sized outdoor tables as part of his Eagle Scout project. Additionally, several people helped to add garden

plots to the existing playground. Maggie, too, found a renewed interest in the grounds of the school campus. Whereas previously she had taken charge of planting flowers in pots outside the main doors, she was now delighted to see children planting seeds in those same pots. They would not see the flowers for months, but the experience made available to the children was authentic and timely. The church also started using the outdoor classroom area for events, which inspired the larger church community to care for nature in new ways, with a specific interest in planting only noninvasive plants on the church property.

Maggie's neighbor who attended the training decided to start a social-media group to help people in the community understand environmental issues. After witnessing children throwing stones at ducks on the nearby water reservoir, instead of shaming the children, she started a junior naturalist group to provide opportunities for children to gather and learn more about their environment. After hearing complaints from neighbors about trees being cut down in the neighborhood, the group provided information on invasive species.

How communities communicate about their environment can make a huge difference in how people identify with the nature in their neighborhood. Community collaboration is integral to the start of an outdoor classroom. People from different backgrounds and experiences come together and do not always agree. In our vignette, Maggie was strategic in recruiting a wide variety of people to be on the task force. The diversity promoted rich conversations about the pros and cons of starting down a new philosophical path. Out of those conversations came a deeper understanding of their beliefs and attitudes about outdoor education.

Questions for Reflection and Action

- ➜ What role will you play as you transform your setting through a nature-based STEM lens?
- ➜ What barriers exist in your setting to either moving to a STEM-focused program outdoors or bringing STEM-focused outdoor projects into the classroom? How will you overcome these barriers?
- ➜ What resources do you need to meet your goals? training? materials? funds?
- ➜ For your community, what are the most important concepts about STEM outdoor learning to communicate? What will be some effective means of communicating that message?

Chapter 8
MAKING THE OUTDOOR CLASSROOM A REALITY

Schools with outdoor classrooms define spaces within their area similar to the way they define spaces in the indoor classroom. Defined spaces are a way to instill structure and develop discipline in children without even talking. An area that is set up for art with paper, paint, and a variety of materials visually calls children to come and create. Similarly, a climbing structure made with logs invites children to climb, balance, and jump. An area with shovels and buckets invites digging, and a blanket with books says, "Let's sit and read." Signs and labels are also an excellent way to help delineate the areas and build literacy skills. The

flexibility in how you approach the boundaries is a personal choice. Think about your centers or learning areas in your preschool classroom. How much more engaging could these areas be in an outdoor setting? Think of your entire outdoor area as the science and/or sensory table and block area.

In comparison to jobs in the classroom, classroom helpers take on a whole new level of interest and skill development outdoors. For instance, the weather helper might be responsible for counting the clouds in the sky, checking how much water is in the rain gauge, or reporting whether the windmill is turning due to the wind. You might designate a compost spinner (someone to crank the compost tumbler) or an equipment monitor who counts to make sure that all the magnifying glasses are returned at the end of the session. The roles are authentic and the work inspires lessons in STEM, all while interacting with the environment. Questions come easily, and rich academic-vocabulary development naturally happens. Typical topics take on a whole new texture and depth in an outdoor setting. The following section shows how you can easily bring your indoor learning areas outside.

Bringing the Indoors Out

The typical preschool classroom offers a variety of spaces and interest areas for children to explore. Let's take a look at ways to provide those opportunities in a rich outdoor setting.

MEETING AREA

The classroom meeting area is usually a large area rug where children can gather to hear a story, have a short whole-group lesson, or sing songs. An outdoor meeting area can consist of blankets on the ground, logs placed in a circle, or weather-proof cushions. If shade is needed, the space can be defined under a tent or tree.

Book Corner

The indoor book corner is usually a cozy space supplied with books in a basket or on a shelf and some comfy pillows to sit on. Children are encouraged to snuggle in alone or with a friend and explore the interesting materials. This center easily transitions to an outdoor setting. You can set up a book "corner" in a tent with some waterproof pillows or spread out a blanket or tarp under a tree. Books can be displayed in a basket or on a log or bench. Teachers find that books are best brought inside each day for dry storage. Just as you would inside, provide fiction and nonfiction books, and rotate them as the themes and interests of the children change. One preschool purchased laminated field guides of local birds, trees, and flowers. These field guides were extremely popular, as they had pictures of nature that the children could possibly match to their environment. Because they were laminated, the guides could be stored in a waterproof box in the outdoor storage unit.

Depending on the location of your outdoor classroom, you might invest in a wagon that you can fill with items that you cannot leave outside overnight. An all-terrain wagon, such as the type one might bring to the beach, is preferable. One teacher of three-year-olds actually instructs them to hold onto the sides of the wagon as they walk. This creative idea helps keep little ones together so that they get to their destination safely.

Block Area

In a classroom, the block area is stocked with manipulatives and wooden blocks of all sizes. The area can be a noisy one, so it is usually set up away from quieter spaces, such as the book corner, and is often defined by shelving and a sound-muffling area rug. Outdoors, the noise of falling block towers is not an issue. The block area can be stocked with wooden blocks of all sizes that are stored in a bin when not in use. Natural materials and loose parts, such as acorns or pine cones, can be added as the seasons change. With a little imagination, a wood pallet in the block area can become a raft. Big sticks can be used as paddles as children sail off to their next adventure.

Boxes are also fun to use in a block area. Like blocks, they can be used to build structures. Big boxes can be perfect places to hide. Be sure to bring them indoors or place them in the recycle bin if the weather looks like rain. Soggy boxes are no fun to pick up!

Dramatic Play

The dramatic play area, that classic preschool center, is typically set up with play kitchen appliances, a child-sized table and chairs, and a variety of pretend food and play utensils. In an outdoor classroom space, a kitchen area can be set up with a tub for a sink, authentic utensils, bowls for mixing, and tree stumps or logs to function as chairs and tables. "Food" can take the form of sticks, leaves, dirt, and other natural materials. Mud pies, anyone? The kitchen area can also take the form of a science lab where experiments take place—after all, cooking and baking are a science!

Truthfully, dramatic play will occur throughout the outdoor classroom and has no boundaries. Children will come up with their own scenarios, often experimenting with words that they have heard and are now trying out in the safe space of pretend play. Often, the play scenarios will mimic parts of real-life experiences and will help children consider what it is like to be someone else, which is an important skill in developing empathy. This can be one of the most joyful times of being a teacher—getting a glimpse into the thoughts of young minds. One teacher overheard a child who was pretending to be a mother telling her appointed "daughter" with utmost authority, "Do your best!"

Sand and Water Tables

Indoors, a water table must be set up on a hard (not carpeted) floor in a spot with easy access to a water source and a sink. The table usually holds an assortment of cups and small containers the children can use to explore the water. Similarly, the sand table is typically set up where fallen sand can easily be swept up and is stocked with an assortment of small sand toys.

Outside, the children can explore water with buckets, watering cans, and sprinklers. They can create "ponds" and "rivers." In warmer months, water play can be a more whole-body experience. Children will use tools to move water from the source to water their plants. A large outdoor area filled with play-grade sand can be stocked with tools that rotate with the themes. For example, during a bridge unit, the area can be full of loose parts for building bridges.

Digging is also a popular activity. Sturdy child-size shovels can be stored in an outside storage container and brought out for daily use. For safety's sake, designate a well-marked digging spot so that small holes are not scattered throughout the area.

Art Center

Similar to a water table, an indoor preschool art area is typically set up in a space where the floor can be cleaned easily and water is accessible. There is usually a table and easels supplied with art materials such as paper, paint, tape, glue, clay, and so on. The outdoors is a source of inspiration for art explorations. An art table and easels can be easily set up outside, where drips and spills are not a big issue. The space can be supplied with the same art materials as are used indoors. Wet projects can be hung on a clothesline or pinned to a fence to dry.

Science Center

Often, a science center in an indoor classroom is a table with shells, rocks, and magnifying glasses. A sensory table may be part of the science center or in an area on its own. A sensory table is often filled with objects to touch, smell, look at, listen to, and taste (under adult supervision). Outdoors, your outdoor science center naturally doubles as your sensory table. An outdoor science area is filled with items to explore that are likely to spark new investigations and learning. Providing a variety of tools, such as magnifying glasses, tweezers, a tablet for recording observations, containers for collecting specimens, binoculars, a thermometer, and so on, lets children investigate the outdoor setting and solve problems. For example, What bird made that noise? How can we examine an insect and return it to its habitat unharmed? What does this flower smell like?

Schedule

Teachers say that time spent in an outdoor classroom seems to fly, especially in mild weather. Schools may have to change their schedules so that children can spend more time outside or so that more classes can use the space. Perhaps a class could hold circle time outside instead of inside. Or a class could save their art project for the outdoor classroom. It will take creativity to plan equal opportunities for all classes. If the outdoor classroom is being used by just one class, there is more flexibility.

Even in the most flexible environment, children will feel safe to explore if they know and understand the routine. Will you offer free play before meeting time or meet first to introduce themes or discuss rules? Will you read a story to the whole class together or read to small groups periodically, as requested by the children? Will the easel be available at all times or be closed some of the time? Where will the children wash hands before eating a snack or lunch? How close are the bathrooms to your outdoor space? How do you plan to dismiss the children? What if a thunderstorm is forecast? Have a few plans in place so that staff knows what to do if changes in weather call for a quick retreat back to the indoor classroom.

Whatever your schedule, stick to the main order of events so that the children and any coteachers or volunteers know what to expect. The goal is to create a flow to the day that makes sense, with as few transitions as possible.

To help you think through how you will expand children's learning to your outdoor space, we have created an outdoor planning sheet (see appendix B). The following is an example, so you can see how it might be filled out.

Name of Unit/Theme: Insects and Spiders in Our World

Shifts for outdoor learning: Children can observe insects and spiders in their original habitats and the effects these creatures naturally have on those habitats. Regular visits over time to the same outdoor area offer opportunities to observe the natural life cycles of insects and spiders.

Main concepts to teach:

1. Insects and spiders are all around us in the natural world. Discovery outdoors will help us learn what types of insects and spiders live near us.

2. Children will explore the characteristics of insects and spiders: What are the basic parts of an insect? of a spider? What do they eat? Where do they live (habitat)? How do they move?

3. Children will compare insects to spiders and discuss ways they are different.

4. Children will compare and contrast the characteristics of insects and spiders to the basic parts of a child, what children eat, where children live, and how children move.

5. Children will learn how insects and spiders can be helpful to humans and how can they be harmful to humans.

Before the unit begins, consider:

→ **What prior knowledge do the children have about insects and spiders?** As an authentic shared writing activity, create a KWL chart with the children. The children can share the pen and either write words or draw pictures. It is okay to record misinformation under "What do we know?" At the end of the unit, this chart will be revisited and we will see if what we thought we knew about insects and spiders is correct.

K: What do we **know**?	W: What do we **want** to know?	L: What did we **learn**?
What do we know about insects and spiders?	What do we want to know about insects and spiders?	What did we learn? Was anything we thought we knew correct? incorrect?
All bugs bite us. Insects and spiders have lots of legs. Bees make honey.	What kinds of insects live in our outdoor area? What do insects eat? How do spiders make webs?	Spiders have eight legs and insects have six. Bees do make honey. Spiders make webs with their spinnerets.

→ **What, if any, additional background knowledge will you, the teacher, need to provide?** After completing the *K* part of the chart, you will know what your students know. You will understand what knowledge to reinforce, what gaps to fill, and what misconceptions need to be corrected.

→ **What do you personally need to learn about insects and spiders? How will you fill the gaps in your knowledge?** You need to fill in your own KWL chart as an adult learner. What do you need to learn about the insects and spiders in your area? The internet and your local librarian are great resources. Here are a few websites to get you started:

Insect Identification
https://www.insectidentification.org
National Geographic: Spiders
https://www.nationalgeographic.com/animals/invertebrates/facts/spiders
The Insect and Spider Collections of the World Website
http://hbs.bishopmuseum.org/codens/

➡ **What will you model or think aloud to support this unit/theme?** After completing the K and L parts of your chart, think strategically about the concepts you will be teaching. What are the more abstract concepts you will need to explain and model?

➡ **What questions will you ask to promote critical thinking about the topic?** (Go from simple to complex.)

- How many legs do spiders have?

- What do bees eat?

- What is the habitat of ticks?

- How can you tell the difference between an insect and a spider?

- Why do bees sting?

- What should we do if we get stung by a bee?

- What problems do insects cause?

- How do insects help us?

- If you were an insect, where would you live? Why?

- What tool could you invent to spin a web like a spider?

Connections to required curriculum

English Language Arts

Oral-language development, Reading foundation skills, Listening comprehension, Fluency, Writing, Academic vocabulary

➡ Engage with a variety of texts (such as a variety of structures and/or genres) with purpose and understanding to support comprehension.

➡ Demonstrate understanding of spoken words, syllables, and sounds (phonemes).

- → Phonological awareness: Recognize rhyming words in spoken language.
- → Writing: With modeling, guidance, and support from adults, review drawing, dictation, or developmentally appropriate writing.
- → Develop academic vocabulary: *insect, spider, arachnid, head, antennae, thorax, abdomen, legs, mouth, wings, web, spinnerets, egg, immature, adult, food, plants, stems, seeds, flowers, prey*

Math

Counting and cardinality, Number names, Counting sequence, One-to-one correspondence, Geometry

Science

- → Demonstrate the thinking and acting inherent in the practice of science.
- → Raise questions about the world around them and be willing to seek answers by making careful observations through discovery.
- → Use scientific skills and processes to explain the interactions of environmental factors (living and nonliving), and analyze their impact from a local to a global perspective.

Fine Arts

- → Demonstrate the ability to organize knowledge and ideas for expression in the production of art.
- → Create images and forms from observation.

Social Foundations

- → Initiate and maintain positive interactions (talking, playing).
- → Play or work with others cooperatively.
- → Through different insights and knowledge, benefit from new reasoning about insects and bugs through play.

Selected books, videos, realia, and visuals to teach new concepts

Narrative literature:

Aardema, Verna. 1975. *Why Mosquitos Buzz in People's Ears: A West African Tale*. New York: Dial Books for Young Readers.

Bunting, Eve. 1999. *Butterfly House*. New York: Scholastic.

Carle, Eric. 1999. *The Very Clumsy Click Beetle*. New York: Philomel.

Carle, Eric. 1995. *The Very Busy Spider*. New York: Philomel.

Dean, James. 2018. *Pete the Cat and the Cool Caterpillar*. New York: HarperCollins.

McDermott, Gerald. 1987. *Anansi the Spider: A Tale from the Ashanti*. New York: Henry Holt.

Moreton, Daniel. 1999. *La Cucaracha Martina: A Caribbean Folktale*. Turtle Books.

Pinczes, Elinor. 1999. *One Hundred Angry Ants*. New York: HMH Books for Young Readers.

Provost, Elizabeth. 2005. *Ten Little Sleepyheads*. New York: Bloomsbury USA.

Yuly, Toni. 2015. *Early Bird*. New York: Feiwel and Friends.

Informational literature:
Gibbons, Gail. 2013. *Ladybugs*. New York: Holiday House.

Gleason, Carrie. 2015. *Everything Insects*. Washington, DC: National Geographic Society.

Marsh, Laura. 2011. *Spiders*. Washington, DC: National Geographic Society.

Mayerling, Tim. 2018. *I See Insects*. New York: Tadpole Books.

McGavin, George. *Insects, Spiders, and Other Terrestrial Arthropods*. Smithsonian Handbooks series. New York: Dorling Kindersley.

Platnick, Norman. 2020. *Spiders of the World: A Natural History*. Princeton, NJ: Princeton University Press.

Rau, Dana Meachen. 2012. *Making Butterfly Gardens*. Ann Arbor, MI: Cherry Lake Publishing.

Sill, Cathryn. 2003. *About Insects: A Guide for Children*. Atlanta, GA: Peachtree Publishing.

Titmus, Dawn. 2018. *Insect and Spiders*. New York: PowerKids Press.

Realia and/or visuals for this theme:
Model of insect and spider, samples/pictures/photographs of real insects (both local and from other areas of the world)
Tools for exploration:
trays, magnifying glasses, tweezers, iPad for taking pictures, journals, observation check sheets, clip boards, white boards, writing materials

Highlight authentic cultural connections (mirrors and windows)

→ **Mirrors (resources that reflect the children in the class) for this unit/theme:**

Make sure to include examples from the background experiences of your students. For example, if you are located in Maryland, include realia and visuals of insects and spiders found in the different regions of Maryland, including where your outdoor space is located. These are mirrors reflecting where you are now. Also include realia and visuals of insects and spiders from the areas your families are from. For example, if you have families from the San Francisco Bay area; the mountainous areas of El Salvador; Brooklyn, New York; and Harare, Zimbabwe, do some research on the insects and spiders in those areas and include realia and visuals of those unique insects and spiders. In the age of the internet this is easy to do (see sample resources above). This will provide mirrors for the children from those areas.

→ **Windows (resources that illuminate the world) for this unit/theme:**

Realia and visuals of insects and spiders found in the different regions of your area, including where your outdoor space is located, are also a window for children on their local area. Also include realia and visuals of insects and spiders from the areas your families are from. This will provide windows on the world for the rest of the class.

Hands-on experiences for this unit/theme (list at least one for each concept to be taught)

→ **Investigative Hunts:** After a safety orientation on insects and spiders, children will explore the outdoor environment using their observational tools. They will record their findings by various means, such as drawing pictures, filling in a check sheet, taking a picture, and so on. The data will be collected as a class.

Under the guidance of the teacher, the children will create charts on various attributes for a given day, number of insects and spiders, insects with wings, various colors, etc. This data can be compared over time.

→ **Movement:** After observing insects and spiders in their own habitats, the children will brainstorm how insects move. With the help of the teacher, the class will create insect/spider movement cards. Each card will contain an icon and word for a movement. For example, a card has the symbol for flying: wings, and when the children see that card they would flap their arms to imitate flying; the word *buzz* is the symbol for buzzing like a bee, and so on. The children can take turns leading the others in moving like insects and spiders.

- **Insect and spider poetry:** As a group, create simple rhyming poems with the insect and spider vocabulary lists. Have the children draw pictures and dictate their own poems to an adult.
- **Outdoor writing center vocabulary list:** Post insect- and spider-related words on a whiteboard. Add to it as the children learn new words. This will support the children's journal writing.
- **Outdoor art center:** Add pictures of insects and spiders to the art center. Children can create artwork and dictate descriptions of what they have made to an adult.

Field trips, guest speakers, and so on to support this unit/theme

A local beekeeper visits the outdoor classroom and explains her equipment and how she collects and processes honey.

Support the families in exploring this unit with their children

In the weekly class blog post over the course of the unit:

- Share the basics concepts you will be teaching in the insect and spider unit.
- Invite families to visit the outdoor classroom and share any information they have about insects and spiders.
- Share the book list and encourage the families to go to the library to check out additional books and videos on insects and spiders.
- Explain how families can make their own outdoor explorations and collect data on insects and spiders.
- Share that the biological sciences department at the local community college has an open house, including a visit to their specimen collection that includes insects and spiders.
- Invite the families to your outdoor space for a Bug Ball. The children can share their artwork, stories, scientific charts, and insect and spider moves.
- Serve "ants on a log" (cream cheese on celery with raisins) and "spider juice." (Let the children invent their own recipe based on what they have learned about spiders.)

How will the class show what they have learned about the topic? How will they share their knowledge with others?

The children will share their understanding of insects and spiders in their daily journals and through weekly insect/spider data check sheets. This will also demonstrate their developing emergent reading and writing skills.

What translations are needed and in what languages?

The first language of three children and their families is Spanish (spoken in El Salvador) and of two children is French (spoken in Haiti).

Conclusion

As we have discovered on our journey through this book, outdoor education, through the lens of STEM and the practice of nature-based education, offers many benefits. You can meet standards, teach required curriculum, and provide opportunities for underrepresented groups to see themselves as fully capable of participating in STEM and, later, STEM-embedded careers. The research shows that the benefits of a STEM-infused outdoor program are many and are important for children to experience. We need to strive for all children to have access and remove barriers to participation.

With your new knowledge of outdoor education and STEM, take a moment and ponder: What are you already doing that is nature-based? How are you already including STEM in your classroom? How can you move what you are doing inside outside? What are your barriers to this type of program? How can you take steps to remove them?

We hope that this book has helped to demystify the basic constructs of STEM and has inspired and empowered you to continue to move to more meaningful and developmentally appropriate learning activities outdoors. Don't be afraid. Remember you do not have to do it all. Any steps you take will benefit children. Outdoor education through a STEM lens is grounded in early childhood theory and can be our way back to the roots of developmentally appropriate practice in the children's garden, where children can grow and flourish.

Appendices

Appendix A: Self-Assessment of the Four Cs

The following self-assessment is meant to help teachers and administrators understand the 21st-century learning and innovation skills in the context of outdoor learning. Teachers may find that a group discussion following the self-assessment can help them focus on ways to be innovative, and, as a group, transform current lessons into more authentic, worthwhile outdoor STEM experiences for young children.

Answer the following questions as honestly as you can.

Communication

→ Am I willing to do more than supervise outdoors?

→ Do I listen to the children in my class while they are playing and exploring?

→ Do I repeat back to children what I hear to be sure that I am understanding them correctly?

→ Do I model the importance of literacy skills to STEM learning by recording what children say and then reading it back to them?

→ Do I practice patience with dual language learners and offer hands-on experiences to communicate concepts?

→ Do I share interesting outdoor discoveries with families and how they align with the state standards?

→ Do I help children understand STEM by narrating their play using STEM words?

Collaboration

→ Do I include children in developing class rules/procedures for the outdoor environment?

→ Do I allow other teachers, families, and community members to help me?

→ Am I purposefully looking to work with people who are not like me so that I get a more diverse viewpoint?

→ Do I allow and encourage children to work together to complete a project?

→ Do I encourage children to ask for help from or offer help to their classmates?

Creativity

→ Do I allow for messes or weather changes by wearing appropriate gear for teaching outside?

→ Have I checked the outdoor space for hazards that could harm children?

→ Do I give children in my class permission to play?

→ Am I able to talk about creativity in STEM?

- Do I know how to transform a lesson to allow for creative expression?
- Do I encourage children to share what they know through art, music, or dance?
- Do I celebrate new construction in the block area, or new creations in the sand box?

Critical Thinking
- Do I show appreciation of new ideas?
- Do I ask open-ended questions?
- Am I open to learning in my personal life?
- Do I show my students how STEM helps us find answers to difficult questions?
- Do I celebrate different ways to get to the same answer?
- Do I model research by looking up questions on the internet in front of children, or talking about a trip to the library?
- Am I willing to grow with the children in my class?
- Is it okay for me not to have all the answers?

Ideas, Beliefs, and Preferences

Circle the answer that best describes your ideas, beliefs, or preferences, and add answers to finish open statements. What do your answers reveal about you?

Teaching STEM
- I feel confident teaching STEM indoors because . . .
- I feel confident teaching STEM outdoors because . . .
- I feel confident teaching STEM indoors and outdoors.
- I do not feel confident teaching STEM because . . .

Play
- I provide playful learning experiences outside and inside.
- I provide playful learning experiences only outside.
- I provide playful learning experiences only inside.

Student Agency
- I prefer to give my students options and allow them to choose from a variety of activities.
- I decide how long to run an activity by observing the children's level of interest.
- I am open to extending a unit if children are interested.
- I prefer to stay with a strict schedule so that I can be sure to have time for everything that I have planned.

Personal Preferences
- I prefer learning indoors.
- I prefer learning outdoors.

→ I prefer using lesson plans that have been tested over time.

→ I prefer trying new lesson plans.

→ I prefer dressing up for teaching because . . .

→ I prefer dressing casually for teaching because . . .

→ I prefer learning with music on.

→ I prefer learning in a quiet setting.

As a child

→ I spent a lot of time playing outside.

→ I spent a little time playing outside.

→ I was not allowed to play outside.

→ How might my past experiences influence my outdoor teaching?

Appendix B: Outdoor Unit Planning Sheet

Name of Unit/Theme:

Topic:

List the main concepts to be taught.

What if any additional background knowledge will you need to provide? What do you need to learn?

Connections to Required Curriculum:

➡ Emphasize academic vocabulary. Words for this unit/theme:

➡ Model and think aloud. What will I model/think aloud to support this unit/theme? What questions will I ask to promote critical thinking about the topic?

➡ Select books, videos, realia, and visuals to teach new concepts.
   - Books/videos for this unit/theme:

   - Narrative/literature:

   - Informational literature:

   - Realia and/or visuals for this unit/theme:

➡ Highlight authentic cultural connections (mirrors and windows).

   - Mirrors (resources that reflect the children in the class) for this unit/theme:

   - Windows (resources that illuminate the world) for this unit/theme:

→ Provide hands-on learning experiences.
  • Hands-on experiences for this unit/theme (list at least one for each concept to be taught):

  • Independent outdoor center experiences to support this unit/theme:

  • Field trips, guest speakers, and so on to support this unit/theme:

→ Seek additional outdoor classroom support. Whom can I ask for help with this unit/theme? How can they help me?

→ Support the families in exploring this unit with their children.
  • How will I support families with this unit/theme (newsletters, online links, books, other resources)?

  • How will the students show what they have learned about the topic? How will they share their knowledge with others?

What translations are needed and in what languages?
→ Schedule of Lessons:
  Week 1
  • Monday:

  • Tuesday:

  • Wednesday:

  • Thursday:

  • Friday:

Appendix C: Resources

WEBSITES

Children and Nature Network https://www.childrenandnature.org
The Children and Nature Network supports a global movement of leaders to turn the trend of an indoor childhood back out to the benefits of nature—and to make sure that all children have equitable access to outdoor spaces where they can learn, play, and grow.

The Forest School Foundation https://www.theforestschoolfoundation.org/
The Forest School Foundation is a nonprofit organization that supports the creation of forest schools in the southeastern United States.

The Irvine Nature Center https://www.explorenature.org
The nonprofit Irvine Nature Center is located in Owings Mills, Maryland, and is the site of an early childhood outdoor classroom that informed the hands-on outdoor learning experiences of the authors.

Maryland Department of Education
For an example of learning and curriculum standards for young children, see the *Maryland Early Learning Standards: Birth–Age 8.*
https://earlychildhood.marylandpublicschools.org/system/files/filedepot/4/ms-de-pedagogy-report-_appendix_2016.pdf

Nature Explore https://natureexplore.org
Nature Explore is a national nonprofit program that provides workshops and conferences, natural products, and design services for the outdoor classroom and offers family connections to nature.

North American Association for Environmental Education https://naaee.org
The goal of NAAEE is to provide excellence in environmental education. The association holds an annual conference to share the latest research in environmental education.

OTHER RESOURCES

Hirschmann, Kris. 2019. *Forest Club: A Year of Activities, Crafts, and Exploring Nature.* London, UK: Quarto Publishing.
Beautifully illustrated by Marta Antelo, this book includes a variety of activities to enhance outdoor learning, along with plenty of nature facts to pique the interest of teachers and students alike.

Two options for outerwear that protects clothing from dirt, mud, plants, and so on:

https://oaki.com/collections/one-piece-suits

https://tuffo.com/muddy-buddy/

References and Related Resources

Adams, Anne, et al. 2014. "Supporting Elementary Pre-Service Teachers to Teach STEM through Place-Based Teaching and Learning Experiences." *Electronic Journal of Science Education* (18)5.

Amelia. 2018. "The Benefits of Play Kitchens for Children." Early Years Resources. https://www.earlyyearsresources.co.uk/blog/2018/05/play-kitchen-benefits/

Ardoin, Nicole M., and Alison W. Bowers. 2020. "Early Childhood Environmental Education: A Systematic Review of the Research Literature." *Education Research Review* 31: 1–16.

Barrable, Alexia, and Liz Lakin. 2020. "Nature Relatedness in Student Teachers Perceived Competence in Willingness to Teach Outdoors: An Empirical Study." *Journal of Adventure Education and Outdoor Learning* 20(3): 189–201.

Alesi, Marianna, et al. 2014. "Improvement of Gross Motor and Cognitive Abilities by an Exercise Training Program: Three Case Reports." *Neuropsychiatric Disease and Treatment.* 10: 479–485. doi: 10.2147/NDT.S58455

Alesi, Marianna, et al. 2016. "Improving Children's Coordinative Skills and Executive Functions: The Effects of a Football Exercise Program." *Perceptual and Motor Skills* 122(1): 27–46.

Battaglia, Giuseppe, et al. 2019. "The Development of Motor and Pre-literacy Skills by a Physical Education Program in Preschool Children: A Non-Randomized Pilot Trial." *Frontiers in Psychology* 9: 2694.

Beery, Thomas, and Kari Anne Jørgensen. 2016. "Children in Nature: Sensory Engagement and the Experience of Biodiversity." *Environmental Education Research* 24(1): 13–25.

Bilton, Helen. 2018. "Values Stop Play? Teachers' Attitudes to the Early Years Outdoor Environment." *Early Child Development and Care* 190(1): 12–20.

Black, Maureen, et al. 2017. "Advancing Early Childhood Development: From Science to Scale 1: Early Childhood Development Coming of Age: Science through the Life Course." *Lancet* 389(10064): 77–90.

Braun, Tina, and Paul Dierkes. 2017. "Connecting Students to Nature—How Intensity of Nature Experience and Student Age Influence the Success of Outdoor Education Programs." *Environmental Education Research* 23(7): 937–949.

Bredekamp, Sue. 2017. *Effective Practices in Early Childhood Education: Building a Foundation.* 3rd ed. Boston: Pearson.

Burry, Madeleine. (2018). "Why Art Was Added to Science, Technology, Engineering, and Math." NYMetroParents. https://www.nymetroparents.com/article/how-stem-became-steam

CAST. 2018. *Universal Design for Learning Guidelines.* Version 2.2. The UDL Guidelines. http://udlguidelines.cast.org

Callcott, Deborah, Lorraine Hammond, and Susan Hill. 2018. "The Synergistic Effect of Teaching a Combined Explicit Movement and Phonological Awareness Program to Preschool Aged Students." *Early Childhood Education Journal* 43(3): 201–211.

Chang, Ya-Ning, et al. 2020. "The Relationships between Oral Language and Reading Instruction: Evidence from a Computational Model of Reading." *Cognitive Psychology* 123: 101336. https://doi.org/10.1016/j.cogpsych.2020.101336

Christenson, Lea Ann, and Jenny James. 2015. "Building Bridges to Understanding in the Pre-K Block Center: A Morning in the Block Center." *Young Children* 70(1): 26–28, 31.

Christenson, Lea Ann, and Jenny James. 2020. "Transforming Our Community with STEAM." *Young Children* 75(2): 6–14.

Collier, Ellie. 2018. "The Kitchen Hierarchy Explained: What Is the Brigade de Cuisine?" High Speed Training. https://www.highspeedtraining.co.uk/hub/kitchen-hierarchy-brigade-de-cuisine/

DeMeulenaere, Michelle. 2015. "Promoting Social and Emotional Learning in Preschool." *Dimensions of Early Childhood* 43(1): 8–10.

Dennis, Samuel, and Christine Kiewra. 2018. "Studying Nature-Based Outdoor Classrooms." *Exchange* 40(2): 72–74.

Dewar, Gwen. 2016. "Learning by Doing: How Outdoor Play Prepares Kids for Achievement in STEM. Natural Start Alliance. https://naturalstart.org/feature-stories/learning-doing-how-outdoor-play-prepares-kids-achievement-stem

Dilek, Hasan, et al. 2020. "Preschool Children's Science Motivation and Process Skills during Inquiry-Based STEM Activities." *Journal of Education in Science, Environment, and Health* 6(2): 92–104.

Duff, Dawna, J. Bruce Tomblin, and Hugh Catts. 2015. "The Influence of Reading on Vocabulary Growth: A Case for a Matthew Effect." *Journal of Speech, Language, and Hearing Research* 58(3): 853–864.

Durlak, Joseph A., et al. 2011. "The Impact of Enhancing Students' Social and Emotional Learning: A Meta-Analysis of School-Based Universal Interventions." *Child Development* 82(1): 405–432.

Early Childhood Today. 2000. "Pioneers in Our Field: John Dewey—Father of Pragmatism." *Early Childhood Today.* Scholastic. https://www.scholastic.com/teachers/articles/teaching-content/pioneers-our-field-john-dewey-father-pragmatism/

Elkind, David. 2015. *Giants in the Nursery: A Biographical History of Developmentally Appropriate Practice.* St. Paul, MN: Redleaf.

Ernst, Julie. 2014. "Early Childhood Educators' Use of Natural Outdoor Settings as Learning Environments: An Exploratory Study of Beliefs, Practices, and Barriers." *Environmental Education Research* 20(6): 735–752.

Erwin, Elizabeth J. 2017. "Transparency in Early Childhood Education: What the West Can Learn from Australia's Focus on Well-Being." *Global Education Review* 4(3): 56–69.

Fernández Santín, Mercè, and Maria Feliu Torruella. 2017. "Reggio Emilia: An Essential Tool to Develop Critical Thinking in Early Childhood." *Journal of New Approaches in Educational Research* 6(1): 50–56.

Fernández-Santín, Mercè, and Maria Feliu Torruella. 2020. "Developing Critical Thinking in Early Childhood through the Philosophy of Reggio Emilia." *Thinking Skills and Creativity* 37.

First Nations Child and Family Caring Society of Canada. 2017. "Indigenous Children, Youth, and Families in the Next 150 Years." *First Peoples Child and Family Review* 12(2): 1–38.

Flores-Koulish, Stephanie. 2019. "John Dewey, 1859–1952, and His Huge Educational Legacy." Lecture. Philosophy, History and Reforms in Education, Fall Semester. Baltimore, MD: Loyola University.

Gardner, Howard. 1983. *Frames of Mind: The Theory of Multiple Intelligences*. New York: Basic Books.

Goff, Lori S. 2018. "Public Elementary School Teachers' Experiences with Implementing Outdoor Classrooms." PhD Diss. Walden University. https://scholarworks.waldenu.edu/cgi/viewcontent.cgi?article=6903andcontext=dissertations

Government of Canada. 2018. *Indigenous Early Learning and Child Care Framework*. Employment and Social Development Canada, Government of Canada. https://www.canada.ca/content/dam/canada/employment-social-development/programs/indigenous-early-learning/1352-IELCC_Report-EN.pdf

Gurholt, Kirsti P., and Jostein R. Sanderud. 2016. "Curious Play: Children's Exploration of Nature." *Journal of Adventure Education and Outdoor Learning* 16(4): 318–329.

Hall, McClellan. 2007. "Mentoring the Natural Way: Native American Approaches to Education." *Reclaiming Children and Youth* 16(1): 14–16.

Haugen, Kirsten. 2019. "Bringing the Benefits of Nature to All Children." *The Active Learner* Spring: 12–13.

Hewlett Foundation. 2013. "Deeper Learning Competencies." Hewlett Foundation. https://hewlett.org/wp-content/uploads/2016/08/Deeper_Learning_Defined__April_2013.pdf

Hirschmann, Kris. 2019. *Forest Club: A Year of Activities, Crafts, and Exploring Nature*. London, UK: Quarto Publishing.

Hovardas, Tasos. 2016. "Primary School Teachers and Outdoor Education: Varying Levels of Teacher Leadership in Informal Networks of Peers." *Journal of Environmental Education* 47(3): 237–254.

Hugo, Taylor. 2021. "Nature's Classroom." *Viking* (September): 13–17.

Huitt, William, and John Hummel. 2003. "Piaget's Theory of Cognitive Development." *Educational Psychology Interactive*. Valdosta, GA: Valdosta State University. http://www.edpsycinteractive.org/topics/cognition/piaget.html

Hunter, Joshua, Cherie Graves, and Anne Bodensteiner. 2017. "Adult Perspectives on Structured vs. Unstructured Play in Early Childhood Environmental Education." *International Journal of Early Childhood Environmental Education* 5(1): 89–92.

Inan, Hatice Z. 2021. "Understanding the Reggio Emilia-Inspired Literacy Education: A Meta-Ethnographic Study." *International Journal of Curriculum and Instruction* 13(1): 68–92.

International Society for Technology in Education. n.d. "Standards for Students." ISTE. https://www.iste.org/standards/for-students

James, V. Angela, Chloe Dragon-Smith, and Wendy Lahey. 2019. "Indigenizing Outdoor Play." Encyclopedia on Early Childhood Development. https://www.child-encyclopedia.com/outdoor-play/according-experts/indigenizing-outdoor-play

Jang, Hyewon. 2016. "Identifying 21st Century STEM Competencies Using Workplace Data." *Journal of Science Education and Technology* 25(2): 284–301.

Johnson, Tony, and Ronald Reed. 2012. "John Dewey." *Philosophical Documents in Education.* 4th ed. New York: Pearson.

Joubert, Ina, and Giulietta Harrison. 2021. "Revisiting Piaget, His Contribution To South African Early Childhood Education." *Early Child Development and Care* 198(7–8): 1002–1012.

Kahn, Peter, Thea Weiss, and Kit Harrington. 2018. "Modeling Child-Nature Interaction in a Nature Preschool: A Proof of Concept." *Frontiers in Psychology* 9: 835.

Karakiş, Özlem, K. 2021. "Relationship Between Professional Engagement, Career Development Aspirations, and Motivation Towards the Teaching Profession of Prospective Teachers." *Participatory Educational Research* 8(2): 308–329.

Karlsson, Anneli B. 2017. "'It Vapors Up Like This': Children Making Sense of Embodied Illustrations of Evaporation at a Swedish School." *International Journal of Early Childhood Environmental Education* 5(1): 39–54.

Kiewra, Christine, and Ellen Veselack. 2016. "Playing with Nature: Supporting Preschoolers' Creativity in Natural Outdoor Classrooms." *International Journal of Early Childhood Environmental Education* 4(1): 70–95.

Kliebard, Herbert M. 2004. *The Struggle for the American Curriculum, 1893–1958*. 3rd ed. New York: Routledge.

Ladson-Billings, Gloria. 2020. "Building Culturally Relevant Schools Post Pandemic." PBS Wisconsin Education. https://www.youtube.com/watch?v=Rr2monteBbo

Larimore, Rachel A. 2018. "Using Principles of Nature-Based Preschools to Transform Your Classroom." *Young Children* 73(5): 34–41.

Lindeman, Karen W., Michael Jabot, and Mira T. Berkley. 2014. "The Role of STEM (or STEAM) in the Early Childhood Setting." In *Learning across the Early Childhood Curriculum*. Advances in Early Education and Day Care, Vol. 17. Bingley, UK: Emerald Group.

Lloyd, Amanda, Son Truong, and Tonia Gray. 2018. "Place-Based Outdoor Learning: More Than a Drag and Drop Approach." *Journal of Outdoor and Environmental Education* 21(1): 45–60.

Louv, Richard. 2021. "Outdoors for All: Access to Nature Is a Human Right." Child and Nature Network. https://www.childrenandnature.org/resources/outdoors-for-all-access-to-nature-is-a-human-right/

Luff, Paulette. 2018. "Early Childhood Education for Sustainability: Origins and Inspirations in the Work of John Dewey." *International Journal of Primary, Elementary and Early Years Education* 46(4): 447–455.

Mahoney, Joseph L., Joseph A. Durlak, and Roger P. Weissberg. 2018. "An Update on Social and Emotional Learning Outcome Research." *Phi Delta Kappan* 100(4): 18–23.

Malone, Karen, and Sarah J. Moore. 2019. "Sensing Ecologically through Kin and Stones." *The International Journal of Early Childhood Environmental Education* 7(1): 8–25.

Marin, Ananda, and Megan Bang. 2018. "'Look it, this is how you know': Family Forest Walks as a Context for Knowledge-Building about the Natural World." *Cognition and Instruction* 36(2): 89–118.

Maryland State Department of Education. 2003. *Maryland Early Learning Standards*. Maryland State Department of Education, Division of Early Childhood Development. https://earlychildhood.marylandpublicschools.org/system/files/filedepot/4/msde-pedagogy-report-_appendix_2016.pdf

McClure, Elisabeth R., et al. 2017. *STEM Starts Early: Grounding Science, Technology, Engineering, and Math Education in Early Childhood*. New York: The Joan Ganz Cooney Center at Sesame Workshop. https://joanganzcooneycenter.org/wp-content/uploads/2017/01/jgcc_stemstartsearly_final.pdf

McLeod, Scott, and Julie Graber. 2019. *Harnessing Technology for Deeper Learning*. Bloomington, IN: Solution Tree Press.

McLeod, Scott, and Dean Shareski. 2018. *Different Schools for a Different World*. Bloomington, IN: Solution Tree Press.

McNair, Lynn J., and Sacha Powell. 2020. "Friedrich Froebel: A Path Least Trodden." *Early Child Development and Care* 191(7–8): 1175–1185.

Melton, Marissa. 2021. "US Ranger on Mission to Attract More African Americans to National Parks." Voice of America. https://www.voanews.com/a/usa_us-ranger-mission-attract-more-african-americans-national-parks/6203926.html

Mika, Carl, and Georgina Stewart. 2018. "What Is Philosophy for Indigenous People, in Relation to Education?" *Educational Philosophy and Theory* 50(8): 744–746.

Moir, Hughes, ed. 1990. *Collected Perspectives: Choosing and Using Books for the Classroom*. 2nd edition. Norwood, MA: Christopher-Gordon Publishers.

Moller, Karla J. 2016. "Creating Diverse Classroom Literature Collections Using Rudine Sims Bishop's Conceptual Metaphors and Analytical Frameworks as Guides." *Journal of Children's Literature* 42(2): 64–74.

Montessori, Maria. 1950. *The Discovery of the Child*. The Montessori Series Vol. 2. M. Joseph Castelloe, trans. The Netherlands: Montessori-Pierson Publishing.

Montessori, Maria. 1972. *The Secret of Childhood*. New York: Ballantine.

Montessori, Maria. 2013. "Nature in Education." *NAMTA Journal* 38(1): 21–27.

Moomaw, Sally. 2012. "STEM Begins in the Early Years." *School Science and Mathematics* 112(2): 57–58.

Moss, Peter. 2016. "Loris Malaguzzi and the Schools of Reggio Emilia: Provocation and Hope for a Renewed Public Education." *Improving Schools* 19(2): 167–176.

National Academies Press. 2013. *Next Generation Science Standards: For States, By States.* Washington, DC: National Academies Press.

National Association for the Education of Young Children. 2014. "NAEYC Early Childhood Program Standards and Accreditation Criteria and Guidance Assessment." Washington, DC: NAEYC. https://s3.amazonaws.com/fwk-int eractives/0Early+Childhood+Studies/Assessments+/EP004/CECS+EP004_ Assessment_Criteria+and+Standards.pdf

National Association for the Education of Young Children. 2019. *NAEYC Early Childhood Program Accreditation Standards and Assessment Items.* Washington, DC: NAEYC.

National Governors Association Center for Best Practices and Council of Chief State School Officers. 2010. *Common Core State Standards.* Washington, DC: National Governors Association Center for Best Practices and Council of Chief State School Officers.

National Research Council. 2012. *A Framework for K–12 Science Education: Practices, Crosscutting Concepts, and Core Ideas.* Washington, DC: National Academies Press.

Natural Start. 2013. "Bright Ideas: Making Mud Kitchens." Natural Start Alliance. https://naturalstart.org/bright-ideas/making-mud-kitchens

Niles, Michael D., and Lisa G. Byers. 2008. "History Matters: United States Policy and Indigenous Early Childhood Intervention." *Contemporary Issues in Early Childhood* 9(3): 191–201.

Okur-Berberoglu, Emel. 2021. "Some Effects of Unstructured Outdoor Plays on a Child: A Case Study from New Zealand." *International Electronic Journal of Environmental Education* 11(1): 58–78.

Pelo, Ann. 2014. "Finding the Questions Worth Asking." *Exchange* 36(1). http://www.childcareexchange.com/article/finding-the-questions-worth-asking/5021550/

Piaget, Jean, and Bärbel Inhelder. 1969. *The Psychology of the Child*. Trans. by Helen Weaver. London: Routledge.

Ramsook, K. Ashana, Janet A. Welsh, and Karen L. Bierman. 2020. "What You Say, and How You Say It: Preschoolers' Growth in Vocabulary and Communication Skills Differentially Predict Kindergarten Academic Achievement and Self-Regulation." *Social Development* 29(3): 783–800.

Reed, Jolene, and Elizabeth L. Lee. 2020. "The Importance of Oral Language Development in Young Literacy Learners: Children Need to Be Seen and Heard." *Dimensions of Early Childhood* 48(3): 6–9.

Redford, Mark. 2013. "Piaget, Vygotsky, and Forest School." Nest in the Woods. https://nestinthewoods.co.uk/piaget-vygotsky-forest-school/

Robertson, Brye. 2019. *Indigenous Ways of Knowing: The Early Learning Perspective*. Association of Early Childhood Educators of Alberta. https://aecea.ca/sites/default/files/Indigenous%20Ways%20of%20Knowing_0.pdf

Rohde, Leigh. 2015. "The Comprehensive Emergent Literacy Model: Early Literacy in Context." SAGE Open: 5(1). https://doi.org/10.1177/2158244015577664

Rosen, Michael, and Helen Oxenbury. 2003. *We're Going on a Bear Hunt*. New York: Aladdin.

Sabet, Michelle. 2018. "Current Trends and Tensions in Outdoor Education." *BU Journal of Graduate Studies in Education* 10(1): 12–16.

Saracho, Olivia N., and Roy Evans. 2021. "Early Childhood Education Pioneers and Their Curriculum Programs." *Early Child Development and Care* 191(7–8): 1144–1151.

Scott, Lee A. 2017. *21st Century Learning for Early Childhood Framework*. Hilliard, OH: Battelle for Kids. http://static.battelleforkids.org/documents/p21/P21EarlyChildhoodFramework.pdf

Shechter, Taly, Sigal Eden, and Ornit Spektor-Levy. 2021. "Preschoolers' Nascent Engineering Thinking During a Construction Task." *Journal of Cognitive Education and Psychology* 20(2): 83–111.

Smith, Cristy S. 2021. "Book Review: *John Dewey's Imaginative Vision of Teaching: Combining Theory and Practice* by Deron Boyles." *Curriculum and Teaching Dialogue* 23(1/2): 309–312.

Son, Seung-Hee, and Samuel J. Meisels. 2006. "The Relationship of Young Children's Motor Skills to Later Reading and Math Achievement." *Merrill-Palmer Quarterly* 52(4): 755–778.

Spring, Joel. 2016. *Deculturalization and the Struggle for Equality: A Brief History of the Education of Dominated Cultures in the United States*. 8th ed. New York: Routledge.

Stine, Matt, and Elisabeth Weinberg. 2018. *Little Chef*. New York: Feiwel and Friends.

Stoll, Julia, et al, 2012. "Young Thinkers in Motion: Problem Solving and Physics in Preschool." *Young Children* 67(2): 20–26.

Strachan, Andrea, et al. 2017. "Early Childhood Educator Perspectives on the First Year of Implementing an Outdoor Learning Environment in Singapore." *Learning: Research and Practice* 3(2): 85–97.

Streelasky, Jodi. 2019. "A Forest-Based Environment as a Site of Literacy and Meaning Making for Kindergarten Children." *Literacy* 53(2): 95–101.

Suggate, Sebastian, Eva Pufke, and Heidrun Stoeger. 2019. "Children's Fine Motor Skills in Kindergarten Predict Reading in Grade 1." *Early Childhood Research Quarterly* 47: 248–258.

Taylor, Heather B. 2019. "From Fear to Freedom: Risk and Learning in a Forest School." *Young Children* 74(2).

Tinkergarten. 2019. "Set Up an Outdoor Kitchen." Tinkergarten. https://tinkergarten.com/activities/build-outdoor-kitchen

Tovey, Helen. 2017. *Outdoor Play and Exploration*. London, UK: Froebel Trust. https://www.froebel.org.uk/training-and-resources/pamphlets

United Nations. 2021. "Indigenous Peoples at the United Nations." United Nations, Department of Economic and Social Affairs, Indigenous Peoples. https://www.un.org/development/desa/indigenouspeoples/about-us.html

Vahey, Phil, Regan Vidiksis, and Alexandra Adair. 2019. "Increasing Science Literacy in Early Childhood: The Connection between Home and School." *American Educator* 42(4): 17–21.

van der Fels, Irene M. J., et al. 2019. "Relations between Gross Motor Skills and Executive Functions, Controlling for the Role of Information Processing and Lapses of Attention in 8–10-Year-Old Children." *PLoS ONE* 14(10): 1–16.

van der Wilt, Femke, Chiel van der Veen, and Sarah Michaels. 2022. "The Relation between the Questions Teachers Ask and Children's Language Competence." *The Journal of Education Research* 115(1): 64–74.

Vygotsky, Lev S. 1978. *Mind in Society: The Development of Higher Psychological Processes.* Cambridge, MA: Harvard University Press.

Wang, Jennifer, et al. 2013. "Ingenuity in Action: Connecting Tinkering to Engineering Design Processes." *Journal of Pre-College Engineering Education Research* 3(1): Article 2.

Warner, Robert P., and Cindy Dillenschneider. 2019. "Universal Design of Instruction and Social Justice Education: Enhancing Equity in Outdoor Adventure Education." *Journal of Outdoor Recreation, Education, and Leadership* 11(4): 320–334.

Webber, Geoff, et al. 2021. "The Terrain of Place-Based Education: A Primer for Teacher Education in Canada." *Brock Education: A Journal of Educational Research and Practice* 30(1): 10–29.

Yurumezoglu, Kemal, and Merve Oztas Cin. 2019. "Developing Children's Observation Skills Using a Fractal Pattern from Nature." *Science Activities* 56(2): 63–73.

Zeng, Nan, et al. 2017. "Effects of Physical Activity on Motor Skills and Cognitive Development in Early Childhood: A Systematic Review." *BioMed Research International* 2017(1): 1–13.

Index